GREAT INNS of AMERICA.

Brick House Publishing Company
Andover, Massachusetts

Library of Congress Cataloging-in-Publication Data

Great inns of America.

Guide to inns that are members of Great Inns of America, Inc.
Includes index.
1. Hotels, taverns, etc.—United States—Directories.
I. Great Inns of America, Inc.
TX907.G6484   1986   647'.9573   86-14690
ISBN 0-931790-72-7 (pbk.)

Printed and bound in Hong Kong by
Mandarin Offset Marketing (H.K.) Ltd

Contents

Preface

In visits to over three hundred town inns, country inns, and historic hotels over the past several years, I have found many small, delightful, high quality inns throughout the United States which more than meet the standards of discriminating and sophisticated travelers. A large number of these inns are members of Great Inns of America, a group of fine, independently owned inns noted for their historic, architectural, epicurean or geographic significance.

There is something special about each of these inns that sets it apart from the standard accommodations of lodging chains. You will find these inns tastefully decorated and effectively run by pleasant people, truly interested in your comfort and in your enjoyment of their facilities.

Each entry in this guidebook provides information about an inn's history, architecture, location, and specialties, together with other interesting facts. In addition, a list of available facilities and activities with identifying symbols is arranged for convenient scanning.

All guest rooms have private baths, though not all have telephones or television sets. (If these features are important to you, by all means ask about them when you make reservations.) Conference planners are invited to ask about the many unusual settings available for meetings.

Complete information about member inns and confirmed reservations are available by telephone from Great Inns of America. Simply dial 800-533-INNS (in Maryland, 800-247-INNS). Our helpful and well-informed agents will be glad to quote room rates and provide any additional information you may ask for, as well as advising you on deposit procedures and acceptability of pets and young children.

We hope that you will enjoy your stays at our Great Inns and would be pleased to hear from you about your experiences. Bouquet or brickbat, please write and tell us.

William E. Gilbert
President
Great Inns of America, Inc.

GREAT INNS
of
AMERICA

LOS OLIVOS GRAND HOTEL

The original Los Olivos Grand Hotel opened on May 1, 1888. Two years later it burned and was replaced by the present hotel, a twenty-one suite, European-style hostelry. The two western-style Victorian woodframe buildings were designed to blend into the setting of rolling hills, oak trees, ranch land, vineyards, and farms of the Santa Ynez Valley.

In one building is the Norby Gallery, which features a collection of original western art, with pieces on loan from private collections as well as the work of contemporary western artists. Also in that building are Remingtons Restaurant, the lobby, three meeting rooms, and ten guest rooms.

A garden and gazebo are nearby. The west wing includes a pool, spa, and eleven guest rooms. In the European tradition, the suite-size rooms are individually decorated, each with a fireplace and living, dining, and sleeping areas.

Los Olivos Grand Hotel
2860 Grand Avenue
Los Olivos, CA 9344

800-533-INNS
In Maryland 800-247-INNS

 A continental breakfast is complimentary. Remingtons serves lunch and dinner, offering gourmet California-French cuisine and a selection of foreign and domestic wines.

 Le Saloon lounge serves cocktails, beer, and wine. A complimentary chilled bottle of local wine is placed in each guest's room upon arrival.

 Conference facilities can accommodate up to fifty people. Audiovisual equipment is state of the art, designed and built into each meeting room.

 Golf may be played by arrangement at either of two courses nearby.

 Fishing and boat rentals are available at Lake Cachuma. Deep-sea fishing charters depart Santa Barbara Harbor on a regular basis. During certain months of the year, whale-watching trips are available.

 Guests may swim in the hotel's outdoor heated swimming pool, or relax nearby in the outdoor whirlpool.

Los Olivos, California

 Cachuma Trails Riding Stable provides trail riding year round.

 Tours of Santa Ynez Valley can be arranged, including visits to wineries and horse ranches.

 Solvang Theatrefest offers summer stock productions, just fifteen minutes away.

 Santa Ynez airport has aviation fuel and rental cars available.

How to get there: From US 101 follow scenic State Route 154 directly to Grand Avenue at Hollister Street in Los Olivos.

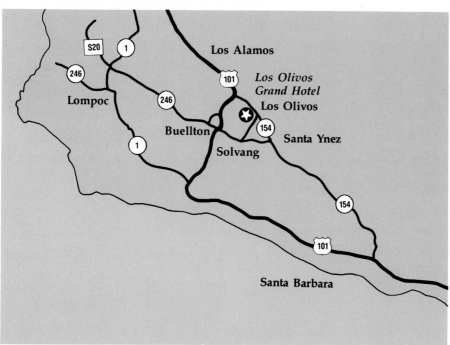

MOUNTAIN HOME INN

Built in 1912 by a homesick Swiss couple, the Mountain Home Inn is located on Mount Tamalpais, the highest peak in the San Francisco Bay Area. The Inn, which offers a spectacular view of the bay, is adjacent to 340,000 acres of parks containing giant redwoods, hiking trails, beaches, and lakes. San Francisco is only twenty minutes away.

Restored in 1985 as a small version of a grand national park hotel, the rustic yet elegant inn embodies classic elements of California design: indoor redwood trees, lots of cedar paneling, warm colors, and windows with sweeping panoramic views.

All ten guest rooms offer attractive views, most have terraces, and several have fireplaces, whirlpools, and skylights. Guests are assured personal attention and service by a large and dedicated staff. The dining room, recognized as one of California's leading restaurants, provides an array of fresh produce and seafood harvested nearby.

Mountain Home Inn
810 Panoramic Highway
Mill Valley, CA 94941

800-533-INNS
In Maryland 800-247-INNS

 Complimentary expanded continental breakfast, lunch, and dinner are served daily, except Monday.

 Beer, wine and aperitifs are served with meals.

 Sailing and windsurfing can be arranged. Surfing lessons and equipment can be rented at shops on the bay and at Muir and Stinson beaches.

 Ocean beaches are five miles down the road at Stinson beach.

 Hiking trails through 340,000 acres of parkland and forest are accessible right outside the inn doors. Since it never snows here, they can be used year round.

 Riding lessons and guided tours through the magnificent ocean parklands are available in nearby Tennessee Valley.

Mill Valley, California

 The inn staff will direct guests to all the local scenic and natural wonders, including Muir Woods, Point Reyes, and Tamales Bay.

 Arts and crafts shops are plentiful in nearby Mill Valley, Sausalito, and Tiburon.

 San Francisco, a major cultural center offering ballet, opera, theatre, and a symphony orchestra, is twenty minutes away.

 September is festival month, with the Mill Valley International Film Festival, Mill Valley Arts Festival, and Mill Valley Wine Festival.

How to get there: Off US 101 north of the Golden Gate Bridge, take State Highway 1, Stinson Beach exit. Turn left at the traffic light (about one half mile) and continue on Highway 1. After two and a half miles, turn right onto Panoramic Highway, continue three miles to the last building on the right before total wilderness.

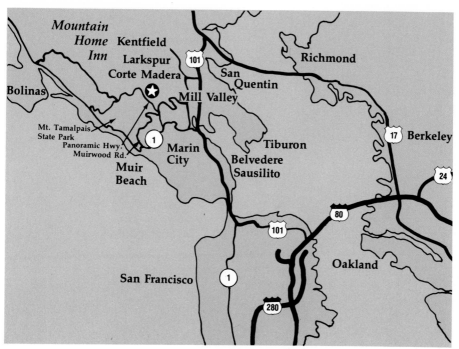

Mountain Home Inn

Los Olivos Grand Hotel ▲ ▼ **Hotel St. Helena**

7

BALBOA INN

The historic Balboa Inn, the Southern California playground for music, movie and political figures of the 1930s and 1940s, has been reborn as a luxurious beachfront hotel.

Located on the Balboa peninsula, where the old Red Car line from Los Angeles once ended at the beach in front of the hotel, Balboa Inn has enjoyed a colorful history, enhanced by its proximity to the Balboa Pavilion and Rendezvous Ballroom, both popular dance spots of the big band era.

While the exterior looks much as former guests Errol Flynn or Glen Miller might remember, the interiors have been upgraded to make them as luxurious as any in Southern California. No two rooms are exactly the same, many have a fireplace, and most feature ocean or bay views.

The three-story inn has ten one-bedroom suites, five mini-suites, and nineteen deluxe guest rooms. Contemporary Mediterranean-style appointments accent the interiors and complement the Spanish Colonial Revival architectural style.

The Grand Suite, a free-standing villa on the second floor, offers a spectacular ocean view from its own private deck and features a living room, master bedroom, two adjoining bedrooms, and three bathrooms with oversized tubs.

Balboa Inn   800-533-INNS
105 Main Street   In Maryland 800-247-INNS
Balboa/Newport, CA 92661

Breakfast is complimentary. California and Continental cuisine, as well as the fresh catch of the day, are featured in The Grill, which overlooks the Pacific Ocean.

The newly redecorated Lounge Bar opens onto the beach and the boardwalk.

Conference groups up to ten can be accomodated in large suites, and up to forty in a fully equipped meeting room.

Sailing, surfing, powerboating, and boat charters for corporate and private parties of up to 150 are available. Catalina Island cruises depart daily. Scuba diving trips may be arranged.

Deep-sea fishing boats with guides are available in the harbor.

Balboa/Newport, California

 Swimming may be enjoyed in the Inn pool. Sand beaches in front of the Inn are among the best in California.

 South Coast Plaza, Fashion Island's designer shops, and the famous farmers' market are all close by.

 Orange County Performing Arts Center offers concerts and many other cultural events throughout the year.

 Orange County Fair, the annual Boat Parade, and the Laguna Beach Art Festival are annual events.

 John Wayne Orange County Airport has aviation fuel and rental cars available.

How to get there: Take State Route 55 until it becomes Newport Boulevard. Continue to Balboa Boulevard and follow signs to The Pier. Balboa Inn is on the corner of Main and Ocean Front at the base of The Pier.

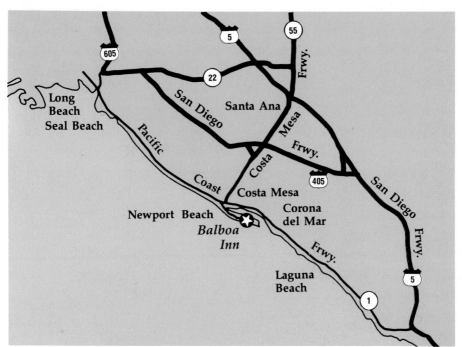

THE UPHAM

The Upham, Southern California's oldest continually operated hotel, was built in 1871 by an adventurous Boston banker. Using redwood timbers and square-headed nails, he built a charming hostelry with sweeping verandas and a cupola, reminiscent of a New England inn. Outside, the gardens offer the feeling of a country retreat, an acre abloom with roses, camelias, and birds of paradise.

The thirty-nine rooms were designed with bold color on the walls, subtle colors in the bath, and soft colors for linens. Each antique bed is topped with a comforter. Fireplaces warm the garden cottages, and a whirlpool bath offers relaxing comfort in the master suite.

Only five minutes' walk from the Inn are the red-tiled attractions of Santa Barbara and its downtown business district. The helpful staff will direct guests to the town's shops, museums, historical treasures, and nightlife, as well as to nearby beaches and mountains.

The Upham
1404 De La Vina Street
Santa Barbara, CA 93101

800-533-INNS
In Maryland 800-247-INNS

 A complimentary continental breakfast is served in the lobby and in the garden veranda, as are afternoon wine and fresh fruit. Lunch and dinner are available in Louie's, a restaurant just off the lobby.

 Louie's features a wine bar with many vintage wines available by the glass.

 Conference groups up to fifty can be accommodated. Audiovisual equipment is available.

 Sailing, surfing, and windsurfing are available in Santa Barbara harbor, just one mile from the inn.

 The Santa Barbara fishing pier is one mile away.

 Mission Santa Barbara, the queen of California missions, is just a few blocks from the inn. Walk to the historic old courthouse, art museum, Arlington theatre, and other museums such as El Paseo.

Santa Barbara, California

 The University of California at Santa Barbara offers cultural and sports events when in session.

 Santa Barbara's specialty shopping district is just two blocks from The Upham.

 The Fiesta del Sol, a week-long street carnival, occurs in midsummer.

How to get there: Leave US 101 at State Street and go north about one mile through downtown Santa Barbara. Turn left on Sola Street, go one and one half blocks to The Upham on the right.

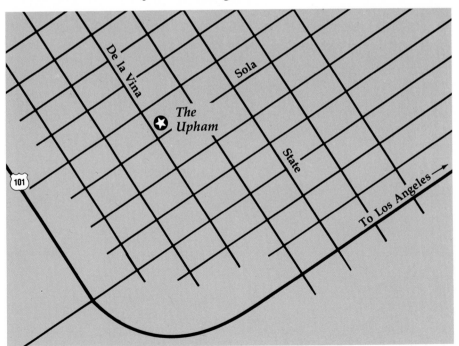

◆ Clocktower Inn ▲ Balboa Inn

Balboa Inn ▼   ▲ The Upham

13

HOTEL ST. HELENA

Hotel St. Helena was established in 1881 as the Windsor Hotel. In its heyday, Lily Langtry is said to have been a frequent guest enroute to her Lake Country residence. Hawaiian royalty chose the hotel as a quiet retreat when visiting the mainland.

The building has been restored and was reopened in 1981. Renewed to its turn-of-the century grandeur, the hotel was granted an award for its significant contribution to Napa county preservation.

The seventeen rooms are furnished with antiques and decorated in tones of burgundy, mauve, chocolate brown, and gold. Carpet and white shuttered windows throughout complement the Victorian touches of brass, hand-carved wood, bent willow, and marble.

In the cooler months, both the lobby and the upstairs sitting room become comfortable havens where guests gather around cozy fireplaces.

From spring through fall harvest, the lobby opens onto a garden court, a relaxing place to linger over complimentary continental breakfast or a glass of the valley's finest wines.

The hotel's courtyard, set in off Main Street, is surrounded by specialty shops filled with fine gifts and classic attire.

Hotel St. Helena   800-533-INNS
1309 Main Street   In Maryland 800-247-INNS
St. Helena, CA 94574

 Complimentary continental breakfast is served each morning in the lobby. Many world-class gourmet restaurants are in the Napa valley and several are within walking distance of the hotel.

 The wine bar, just off the lobby, offers dozens of vintage wines by the glass, and well as cheeses and beer from around the world.

 The entire hotel can be reserved for a single conference rate, with meetings held in the wine bar.

 Vineyard and winery tours abound in the Napa valley. Many excellent boutique wineries are just a short drive from St. Helena, as are some of the larger wineries such as Sabastiani and Gallo.

St. Helena, California

 The historic Silverado Wine Museum is within walking distance of the hotel.

 Quality shops dot Main Street all through St. Helena. Several are reached through the hotel lobby courtyard.

 Hot-air ballooning and soaring are available at the Calistoga airport, fifteen minutes north of St. Helena.

How to get there: From San Francisco, follow Interstate 80 to State Route 29 in Vallejo. Continue north on 29 for thirty-eight miles to St. Helena. The hotel is in the center of town.

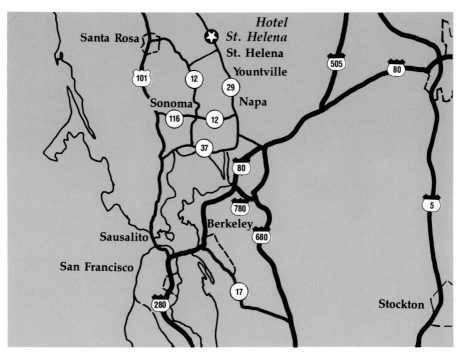

CLOCKTOWER INN

The Clocktower Inn, once a Spanish-style firehouse and landmark clocktower, was remodeled to capture the Spanish influence and architectural heritage of the American Southwest.

The inn's lobby is now a gallery adorned with fiber wall hangings, specially commissioned paintings of Indian villages, and dramatic watercolor abstracts. Santa Fe style furniture, a fireplace with hearth seating, exposed beam ceilings, and red-tiled floor capture the feeling of California's past.

Two newly built wings house fifty rooms, each designed in the tradition of the southwest. Rooms feature paneled doors and windows with wide tile sills deepset for the look of a thick adobe wall.

Some rooms have fireplaces and separate tiled entryways, and most have a private balcony or patio. Each is furnished in quiet desert tones with handmade Santa Fe style headboards and armoires.

Located in the historical heart of Ventura, adjacent to the Mission San Buenaventura, the Clocktower Inn is at the center of a beautiful park setting.

Clocktower Inn
181 East Santa Clara Stree
Ventura, CA 93001

800-533-INNS
In Maryland 800-247-INNS

 Complimentary continental breakfast is served in the glass-domed atrium, and wine and cheese are served at fireside in the lobby. The Rio Grande offers fine Mexican dining.

 The inn's conference room is suited to groups of forty or less. Breaks can be taken in the atrium, and meals are served on the outdoor patio most of the year. The inn hosts only one meeting at a time, so personal service is guaranteed.

 Windsurfing, boating, and cruises to Channel Islands National Park are available in Ventura Harbor, five miles from the inn.

 Swimming and surfing are just two blocks away at the beach.

Ventura, California

 Old San Buenaventura boasts a large variety of historical attractions. From the inn, guests may walk to the Ortega Adobe, the Old Mission San Buenaventura, and the Ventura County Historical and Archeological Dig.

 An interesting mix of shops includes many thrift stores and antique shops interspersed with art galleries. Most are within walking distance of the inn.

How to get there: From US 101 in Ventura, take Ventura Avenue north for two blocks, and turn right onto Santa Clara Street. The Clocktower Inn is on the left at the end of the Mission Park block.

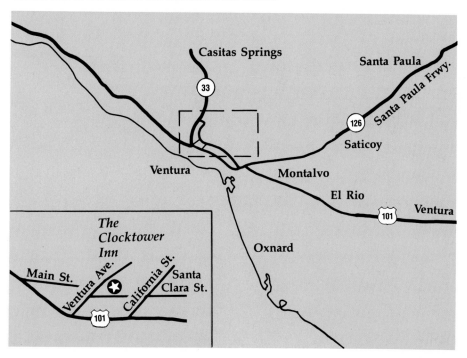

GOLDEN ROSE HOTEL

Restored to its original Victorian elegance, the Golden Rose Hotel is situated in the center of the old gold-mining town of Central City. Built in 1874 and set amid sites of abandoned gold mines, historic homes, and mountain scenery, the hotel is a model of period elegance.

Central City was long known as the richest square mile on earth, after John Gregory discovered gold there in 1869. It was the first and richest gold strike in Colorado. The hotel, its restaurant The Teller House, and Central City itself are all listed on the National Register of Historic Places.

From the concierge's front desk to the parlor with comfortable conversation areas, fireplace, antiques, and appointments, and past the library hot tub and sauna, guests go up the grand staircase to twenty-six pleasing suites and rooms.

The hotel's authentic furnishings are enhanced by silk-screened wall coverings that recreate period patterns, and marble floors and brass fixtures preserve a Victorian flair in the luxurious and up-to-date bathrooms.

The Golden Rose is home to many opera lovers during the summer opera festival, and just down the street, guests may visit bars and shops much as they were a hundred years ago.

Golden Rose Hotel
102 Main Street
Central City, CO 80427

800-533-INNS
In Maryland 800-247-INNS

 Teller House, owned by the hotel and only a few steps up the street, serves breakfast, lunch, and dinner.

 Full bar and fine wines are served at the Teller House on the outdoor terrace overlooking the opera house gardens, and in the Face on the Barroom Floor bar.

 For conferences, the Eureka Ballroom accomodates 200 and can be subdivided for smaller groups. The ballroom has an outside balcony and access to the terrace overlooking the opera house gardens.

 Cross-country skiing gear is available from a local outfitter and transportation is furnished to and from the hotel lobby. Several downhill ski areas are an hour away. Snowshoeing is also available.

 Some of Colorado's most beautiful streams and mountain lakes are nearby.

Central City, Colorado

 Guided trail rides from two outfitters just north of the hotel are available in the summer months.

 The Teller House Museum is open to the public year round. Also available are tours of the gold mines and of the Central City Historical Museum.

 Every Friday and Saturday night, the Little Kingdom Players perform works of such master playwrights as Chekhov and Shaw, to create a memorable dining and entertainment experience.

 The Central City Opera Festival runs six weeks in the summer. The Mining and Milling Festival runs the first part of June. The Central City Jazz Festival runs four days in August. The Gilpin County Arts Festival runs all summer.

How to get there: Take Interstate 70 west from Denver about 45 minutes to the US 6 exit. Follow US 6 east to State Route 119, then follow 119 to the town of Black Hawk. Turn left off 119 and follow the signs to Central City.

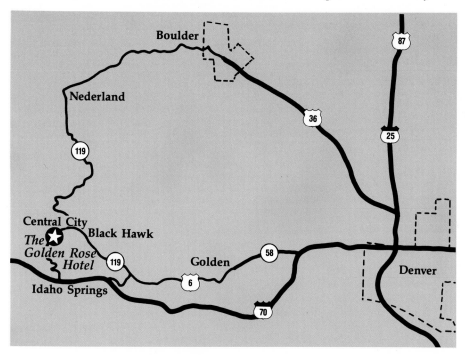

Golden Rose Hotel ⬍

Hearthstone Inn

HEARTHSTONE INN

The Queen Anne building now known as the Hearthstone Inn was built in 1885 as a private home for the family of Judson Moss Bemis. Colorado Springs, at the base of Pike's Peak, was young then, and the occupants of the mansion have watched the town grow from a railroad town to a major aerospace center.

After passing from the Bemis family, the house was used as an apartment building until 1977, when it was rescued from further deterioration. The result is an inn with its original fireplaces, staircases, and woodwork, completely furnished with antiques from the turn of the century.

Three of the twenty-five guest rooms have a private porch, and three have working fireplaces. Each room is individual in color, decor, and feeling, featuring the casual elegance of brass fixtures and burnished walnut. In keeping with the style of the 1880s, there are no phones and no television to mar the quiet and romantic atmosphere.

Guests may enjoy a game of croquet on the lawn, or read on the veranda. The inn is located on a residential street near the center of town, with fine restaurants, shopping, and other attractions only blocks away.

The inn is listed on the National Register of Historic Places.

Hearthstone Inn   800-533-INNS
506 North Cascade Avenue   In Maryland 800-247-INNS
Colorado Springs, CO 80903

 Guests are treated to full gourmet breakfast each morning in the dining room. Luncheons and dinners can be arranged for groups of twenty or more.

 Small group meetings of ten to twenty-five can be accommodated in the dining room around four large tables.

 Public golf courses are a ten-minute drive from the inn.

 Public tennis courts are within walking distance of the inn.

 Directly back of the inn, a magnificent jogging path winds through the city park and behind many lovely mansions.

Colorado Springs, Colorado

 The inn staff will arrange tours of the entire area, including the Air Force Academy, Pike's Peak, the Cripple Creek gold mining district, Cave of the Winds, and the National Olympic Training Headquarters.

 McAllister House museum, other museums, and historic homes and churches are within walking distance. Fort Carson and the Museum of the Army of the West are south of town.

 Colorado College is three blocks from the inn. Also in town is the University of Colorado at Colorado Springs.

 Old Colorado Springs, a restored area of antique shops, boutiques, and charming small restaurants, is a ten-minute drive from the inn.

How to get there: From Interstate 25, take exit 143, Uintah Street east, away from the mountains, and travel three blocks to Cascade Avenue. Turn right on Cascade, continue south for seven blocks, and discover the Hearthstone to the right on the corner of Cascade and St. Vrain.

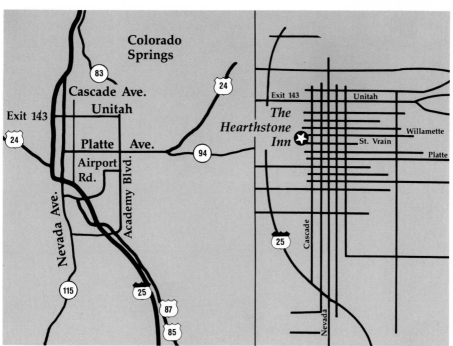

LAKESIDE INN

The recently restored Lakeside Inn recreates the ambiance of the best of the 1930s, an era of old Southern Florida hospitality. The inn is situated on nine acres directly on the shores of Lake Dora.

The original structure, Alexander House, built in 1882 as an inn, is now part of the main building. The architecture of the inn is essentially Tudor, but the inn was built over a period of a hundred years, giving each building a personality of its own.

The eighty-five guest rooms and the public spaces are period showcases for the subtle colors of designer Laura Ashley. The galleried front porch, with its array of rockers and bamboo furniture, looks over terraced lawns to a wide beach.

Mount Dora itself has been described as everyone's idea of Smalltown, USA. Although only an hour's drive from such major attractions as Walt Disney World and Epcot Center, the Lakeside Inn is a tranquil escape into a less hectic past world.

Lakeside Inn
100 North Alexander Street
Mount Dora, FL 32757

800-533-INNS
In Maryland 800-247-INNS

 The Beauclaire, a full-service restaurant, is open every day. Room service is available, as are banquet rooms that cater to groups of up to one hundred and twenty-five for private luncheons and dinners.

 A full-service lounge is open every day, as is a pool bar by the lake.

 For groups of fifteen to forty, executive conference rooms with natural light, private entrances, and a lake view create a pleasant working atmosphere.

 Three golf courses are conveniently near the inn.

 The inn has four lighted tennis courts on the grounds.

 Boating, sailing, windsurfing, and jet skiing are all available, by arrangement.

Mount Dora, Florida

 A heated, olympic-size swimming pool is near the beach.

 The inn has exercise rooms for men and women.

 The Ice House Theatre presents five plays during its season, October through mid-May.

 The annual Mount Dora Art Festival is held in February. A sailboat regatta is featured in March, and the spring Antique Car Tour is an April attraction.

How to get there: From Interstate 4, follow US 441 twenty-two miles northwest of Orlando to the center of Mount Dora.

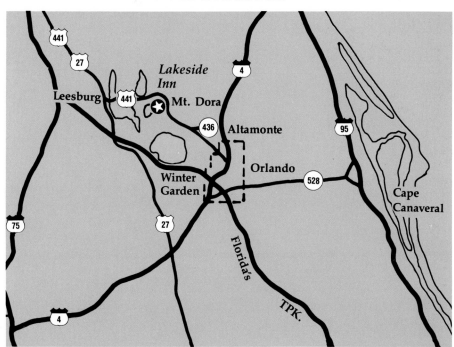

CASA DE SOLANA

Casa de Solana is a lovingly renovated colonial home in the heart of St. Augustine's historical area. It is named for its earliest known occupant, Don Manuel Solana, a direct descendant of the first white settler born in America.

A Spanish dragoon and resident of St. Augustine at the time of the signing the Treaty of Paris in 1763, by which Spain ceded Florida to England, Solana remained in the city to settle real-estate claims for the departing Spanish residents.

The house, which predates the historic 1764 Puente map of the city, is built of coquina blocks, the same material used to construct the Castillo de San Marcos, and is faced with scored stucco. It still has the original hand-hewn beams supporting one of its balconies.

There are four antique-filled guest suites designed for modern convenience without distraction from the accumulated ambiance of two-hundred-and-twenty years. Some have fireplaces, and others have balconies with a breathtaking view of Matanzas Bay.

The large formal dining room boasts a ten-foot mahogany table, and a fireplace designed as a replica of the fireplace in the Oval Office of the White House.

Guests may relax in a walled garden of tropical plants surrounding a stone patio and fountain, and the inn is within easy walking distance of the many attractions of St. Augustine.

Casa de Solana   800-533-INNS
21 Aviles Street   In Maryland 800-247-INNS
St. Augustine, FL 32084

Complimentary full breakfast is served in the inn's formal dining room each morning. Other meals may be taken at one of many excellent restaurants in St. Augustine.

The City Yacht Pier on Matanzas Bay, which is part of the Intracoastal Waterway, is only one block from the inn.

Deep-sea charter boats are available nearby for half and full-day excursions. Excellent fresh-water fishing is also available within one hour's drive of the city.

Ocean swimming from wide, beautiful sandy beaches is less than five miles away.

The inn provides bicycles for touring the city. There are also horse-drawn carriages and tram tours of the historic area. Many attractions are within easy driving distance

St. Augustine, Florida

 The oldest city in the United States, St. Augustine is the locale of the oldest residence, Castillo San Marcos, the oldest school house, and many other buildings dating from the 18th and 19th centuries.

 Flagler College, a four-year coeducational liberal arts college, is housed in the former Ponce de Leon Hotel. The hotel was built in 1888 by Henry Flagler to be the finest of a series of hotels along the east coast of Florida.

 Cross and Sword, the official state play, is presented each summer from mid-June through August in an outdoor amphitheatre. Also during the year several groups of professional performers present their impressions of life in St. Augustine in years gone by.

 Twice a year, on Palm Sunday weekend and Thanksgiving weekend, the city hosts a sidewalk arts and crafts show in the downtown plaza.

 The Municipal airport has aviation fuel and rental cars available.

How to get there: Leave Interstate 95 at US 1, and continue to King Street, State Route 214. Go east on King Street to Aviles Street, and turn right. The inn is on the corner of Cadiz Street, just past Artillery Lane.

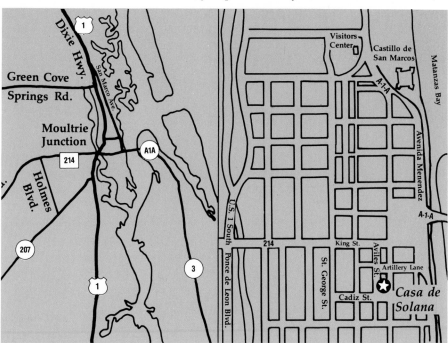

1842 INN

Named for the year it was built, the 1842 Inn was originally the residence of a prominent Macon citizen, John Gresham, and has been restored to its original Greek revival grandeur. The inn is located in the heart of an historic district of Macon. Known as the ante-bellum heart of the South, the city boasts more white-columned buildings than any other city in the United States.

A Victorian-era cottage shares a courtyard with the main house. Together, the two buildings provide twenty-two spacious guest rooms, all furnished with handmade carpets, antiques, and fine reproductions. Although ceiling fans and functional fireplaces add to the ambiance, the inn is centrally air-conditioned and heated. Some of the ample baths feature whirlpools and a second television set.

The 1842 Inn is listed on the National Register of Historic Places.

1842 Inn   800-533-INNS
353 College Street   In Maryland 800-247-INNS
Macon, GA 31201

 A complimentary breakfast is provided, and excellent restaurants for other meals are within walking distance.

 Wine and liquor are served in the public rooms and by room service.

 Conference groups up to twenty-five can be accommodated, and audiovisual equipment is available.

 Lake Tobesofkee provides swiming, numerous white sand beaches, beautiful scenery, fishing, and sailing.

 Horse-drawn carriage and van tours are available year round.

 Fine antebellum residences, significant public buildings, and the 1200-year-old Ocmulgee Indian Mounds are open year round.

Macon, Georgia

Mercer University and Wesleyan College have many cultural events open to the public.

The Grand Opera House, Municipal Auditorium, and Coliseum feature professional performances and events. The Macon Little Theatre and the colleges offer additional entertainment.

The Cherry Blossum Festival occurs the third week in March when the city's fifty-thousand Yoshino cherry trees bloom. White Columns and Holly is a three-week December festival with daily events.

Macon's airport, ten miles south of town, has aviation fuel and rental cars available.

How to get there: Leave Interstate 75 at exit 52, Hardeman Avenue and Forsyth Street. Go east on Forsyth to the second traffic light, and turn left onto College Street. The inn is in the third block on the left.

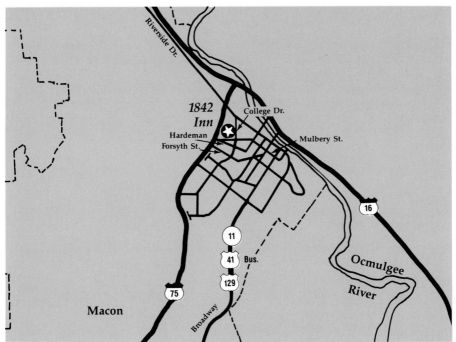

FOLEY HOUSE INN

In 1733, General James Oglethorpe signed a treaty with Yamacraw Indian chief Tomochichi, which allowed English colonists to lay out a city in a series of squares along the forty-foot bluff of the Savannah River. These lovely squares, with their live oak trees and Spanish moss, are an integral part of Savannah today.

One of these squares, Chippewa, is just outside the front door of Foley House Inn. Built in 1876 as two adjoining townhouses in the heart of Old Savannah, the inn was completely restored in 1982. Every cornice, joist, and sill, down to the most minute detail, has been faithfully renewed by master craftsmen.

The furniture, silver, china, Oriental rugs, and hand-colored engravings in the inn's twenty rooms have been carefully selected from around the world, making each room an individual masterpiece, but not entirely old-fashioned: many of the rooms have oversized whirlpool baths.

The time-honored privileges of the innkeeper are faithfully assumed. Upon arrival, guests are served tea in the parlor from a sterling service, wine and evening cordials are served on request, beds are turned down in the evening (with mints on the pillow), and shoes are polished and ready at the door before breakfast.

Foley House Inn   800-533-INNS
14 West Hull Street   In Maryland 800-247-INNS
Savannah, GA 31401

 A continental breakfast is served in the guest rooms or in the courtyard. For other meals, many fine restaurants are a few blocks away.

 Wine, liquors, afternoon specialty drinks, and after-dinner drinks are complimentary.

 Ocean beaches are to be found at Tybee Island, a half hour away, and at Hilton Head Island, an hour away.

 Historic Savannah, Inc., offers many excellent tours of the historic district, as well as to outlying areas.

 The historic district and the many lovely squares and houses are interesting to see. Revolutionary and Civil War sites abound. The restored River Street area and Factors Walk are close by the inn.

Savannah, Georgia

 Local crafts and import shops are among the special attractions of the River Street shopping areas.

 Festivals are a continuous affair in this festive city, including the blessing of the fleet during the last week of June, Octoberfest on Riverfront Plaza during the first week of October, St. Patrick's Day parade on March 17, and the garden tour during April.

How to get there: Interstate 16 dead ends at Montgomery Street. Continue north on Montgomery six blocks to Oglethorpe Avenue. Turn right onto Oglethorpe and go four blocks. Turn right onto Bull Street and go one block. Then turn right onto Hull Street. Foley House Inn is the third building on the right.

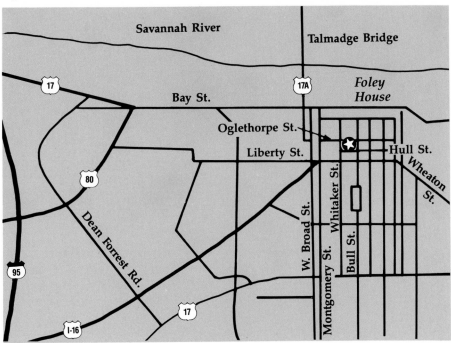

1842 Inn ▲   ▼ Casa de Solana

Soniat House ▼ **Redstone Inn**

33

REDSTONE INN

Redstone, a twenty-three room duplex, was built in 1894 by pioneer industrialist Augustin Cooper as a wedding gift for his daughter Nell. The side occupied by Nell and her husband, Dan Sullivan, was a grand Victorian home of turrets, porches and nooks, with maple and oak woodwork, beveled, leaded and stained glass windows, marble and tiled fireplaces, and crystal-shaded gas lamps.

In 1984 the Redstone was bought by a local group of businessmen and conservationists who converted it into an elegant fifteen-room inn, a blend of Victorian ambiance and modern conveniences, furnished with antiques and steeped in history.

The inn is listed on the National Register of Historic Places, and surrounded by three of the five historic districts in the river city of Dubuque, the oldest city in Iowa and rich in architectural heritage and local history.

Redstone Inn   800-533-INNS
504 Bluff   In Maryland 800-247-INNS
Dubuque, IO 52001

 Complimentary continental breakfast and English afternoon tea are served each day. Groups may reserve luncheons and dinners catered from the inn's own selection of seasonal specialties.

 Alcoholic beverages are served in the parlor and the dining room. Featured are Restone private-label wines, produced and bottled in the area.

 Meetings of groups up to twelve are held in the conference room.

 Downhill and cross-country skiing are available within ten miles. Five Flags Civic Center, one block from the inn, offers ice-skating and professional hockey games.

 The F. W. Woodward Riverboat Museum and William M. Black Sidewheeler Museum are a few blocks from the inn.

Loras College, Clarke College and the University of Dubuque offer a wide range of cultural and sports events.

Dubuque, Iowa

 The inn is located in the Cable Car Square shopping district. Many specialty shops are clustered at the foot of the one-hundred-and-eighty-nine-foot-high Fenelon Place elevator, which affords a spectacular view of the Mississippi River and three states.

 Dubuquefest, the largest Iowa arts festival, is held during the third week in May. Riverfest, focusing on river history, occurs during the third weekend in September. Winterfest is an event in late January.

How to get there: Enter Dubuque on US 20 or US 61/151, follow US 61/151 to Fifth Street and turn west. Redstone Inn is on the right in the first block.

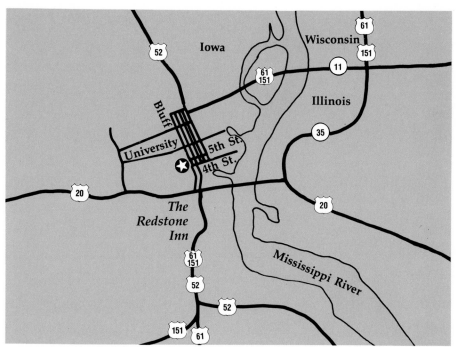

HOTEL MAISON DE VILLE

Hotel Maison de Ville, once a private home, is located in the center of the historic French Quarter of New Orleans. The main house burned down and was rebuilt in the 19th century, but the servants quarters date to 1743. In the twenty-six units of the inn, antique 18th century four-poster double beds and contemporary king-size beds are combined with period furniture, marble basins and brass fittings.

One and a half blocks away but also part of the inn are the Audubon Cottages, named for the celebrated American naturalist. One of the cottages is his "little house on Dauphine Street," where he lived while working on the now-famous *Birds of America.*

The Santo Domingo-style cottages are made of *briquette-entre-poteaux,* or bricks between posts, the Creole version of the half timber houses of Europe. The chrome orange bricks are hand made of Mississippi river clay, and covered with stucco.

Each cottage has a private patio and fountain, opening on to a central courtyard with a swimming pool and pavilion. In the secluded patio of the main house, semitropical plants bloom against a backdrop of wrought-iron gates and brick walls, and water flows slowly over a triple-tiered cast-iron fountain into a fish pond in the center of the courtyard.

Hotel Maison de Ville   800-533-INNS
727 Toulouse Street   In Maryland 800-247-INNS
New Orleans, LA 70130

 Complimentary continental breakfast is served in the guest rooms.

 Full bar service is available.

 Meetings for groups up to twelve can be held in a cottage, and audiovisual equipment is available.

 A private swimming pool is the centerpiece of the Audubon Cottages courtyard.

 Tours of the French Quarter, restored plantations, the Mississippi River, and bayou country are readily available.

 New Orleans Historic District has many buildings and monuments of note.

New Orleans, Louisiana

 Tulane and Loyola Universities provide events of cultural and sporting interest in season.

 The shops of the French Quarter offer a vast assortment of fine antiques and fashionable clothes.

 The French Quarter Festival is held in mid-April. A jazz festival occurs the last weekend of April and the first weekend of May, and the famous Mardi Gras is celebrated in the winter.

How to get there: Leave Interstate 10/US 90 at Exit 236A or 236B and drive south. Turn left onto Toulouse Street and continue south. The inn is on the left, just past Bourbon Street.

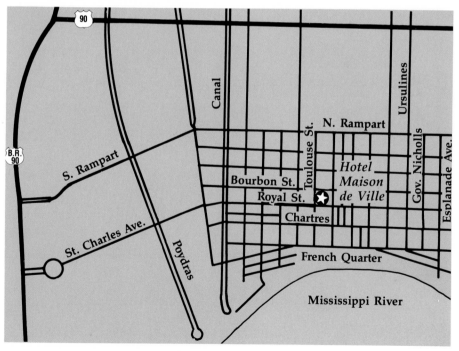

SONIAT HOUSE

Soniat House is situated in a quiet corner of the historic French Quarter. A typical but sumptuous Creole house, it was built in 1830 by a cotton planter, Joseph Soniat Dufossat. In 1982 it was restored by Rodney Smith and furnished with antiques collected by Mr. Smith throughout Louisiana and in England and France.

The inn has twenty-two rooms and a staff of twelve offering deluxe service, orchestrated by a concierge on duty from early morning until midnight. The building and grounds are closed to all but guests and their friends, and guests are given a key to the front gate upon arrival.

Although located in a quiet byway, the inn is only a few blocks from the colorful French Market, Jackson Square, and the riverfront promenade. For business travelers, a limousine ride to the business district is available each morning.

In 1983 the inn won the Vieux Carre award for best restoration, and has been placed on the National Register of Historic Places.

Soniat House   800-533-INNS
1133 Chartres Street   In Maryland 800-247-INNS
New Orleans, LA 70116

 A New Orleans continental breakfast is served in the room, on the room balcony, or on the patio by the lily pond. Room service, from a menu based on recipes handed down from the Soniat family, is available twenty-four hours a day.

 A fully stocked honor bar is always open on the patio.

 Conference groups of up to eighteen can gather in the meeting room.

 Deep-sea fishing out of Empire, Louisiana, can be arranged in advance.

 Tours of the French Quarter, restored plantations, the Mississippi River, and bayou country are available.

New Orleans, Louisiana

 Four historic French Quarter homes are open Monday through Friday from 10 a.m. to 4 p.m.

 The inn is just one block from the famous antique shops of Royal Street.

 The French Quarter Festival is held in mid-April. A jazz festival occurs the last weekend of April and the first weekend of May, and the famous Mardi Gras is celebrated in the winter.

How to get there: Leave Interstate 10/US 90 at Exit 236A or 236B and go south to Rampart Street. Turn left, go nine blocks and turn right onto Esplanade Avenue. Continue six blocks and turn right onto Decatur Street. Go three blocks and turn right onto Ursuline Street. Go one block and turn right onto Chartres Street. Soniat House is on the left.

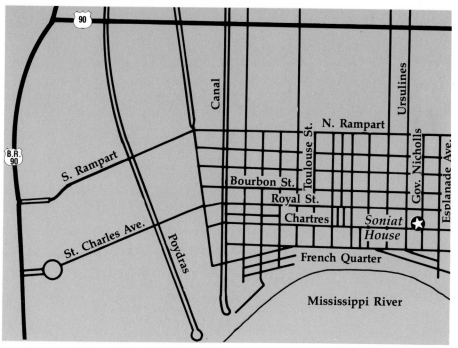

PHENIX INN

Bangor, the "Queen City" of Maine, is the commercial, financial and cultural center of the northeastern part of the state. The Phenix Block, built in 1873, was part of the West Market Square Block of downtown Bangor, since rehabilitated and made part of a National Historic District.

Within the Phenix Block is the Phenix Inn. From the leather furniture of the lobby to the solid mahogany beds in the thirty-seven rooms, the ambiance of the inn was created to be in character with the restored old commercial building.

Phenix Inn   800-533-INNS
West Market Square   In Maryland 800-247-INNS
Bangor, ME 04401

 Continental breakfast is served in the fourth-floor coffee shop. For other meals, there are many excellent restaurants nearby.

 The conference room accommodates groups up to twenty.

 Katahdin Cruises operate summer tours of Penobscot Bay. The inn is located in the center of Bangor's Historic District, making walking tours easy.

 Bangor Historic G.A.R. Museum, Penobscot Heritage Museum, Old Town Historical Heritage Museum, and the University of Maine Anthropology Museum are within a few minutes drive.

 The University of Maine at Orono and Bangor campuses offer many cultural and sports events when in session.

 Bangor's downtown specialty shops are close to the inn.

Bangor, Maine

 Penobscot Theatre, Bangor Symphony Orchestra, Community Concert Association, and Opera New England offer entertainment year round.

 Bangor is home to the State Fair, harness racing, and many other summer festivals.

 Bangor International Airport is two and a half miles from the downtown district.

How to get there: From Interstate 95 take Interstate 395 to Main Street, north. At the sixth traffic light, make a sharp right turn. The inn is just behind a small park.

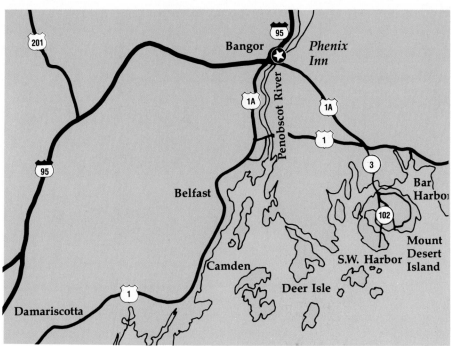

CAPTAIN LORD MANSION

The Captain Lord Mansion is a romantic, faithfully restored Maine coast inn.
Built in 1812 as a private residence by wealthy shipbuilder Nathaniel Lord, the
Federal style mansion has sixteen spacious and luxurious guest rooms.
Eleven of the rooms have working fireplaces.

Each guest room has been individually decorated to reflect the warmth and
charm of an elegant private home. Each room is appointed with reproduction
period wallpaper, an antique bed, a firm posturepedic mattress, color
coordinated linens, and other amenities. In keeping with the relaxed
atmosphere, there are no telephones and no television sets in the rooms.

The inn is situated in a park-like setting in the historic residential area of
Kennebunkport, overlooking the Kennebunk River and a five-minute walk
from Dock Square, with its many shops and restaurants. One mile away is the
rockbound Maine coast and the Atlantic ocean.

Captain Lord Mansion   800-533-INNS
Box 800   In Maryland 800-247-INNS
Kennebunkport, ME 04046

 A complimentary breakfast consists of home baked breads, eggs,
coffee and a variety of herbal teas. Other meals may be taken in the
many excellent restaurants within a mile of the inn.

 Groups of up to twelve can be accommodated in the large gathering
room with fireplace. Audiovisual equipment is available.

 Two eighteen-hole courses are within one mile of the inn.

 Windsurfer rentals are available on the Kennebunk River in front of
the inn.

 Several deep-sea fishing boats run daily from Kennebunkport during
the summer and fall.

 Three white-sand beaches for ocean swimming are within a short
drive of the inn.

Kennebunkport, Maine

 Rachel Carson wildlife refuge, with hiking trails, is off State Route 9 near the inn.

 Kennebunkport Historic District, with many fine old houses, surrounds the inn.

 Ogunquit Playhouse Summer Theatre is fifteen miles south of the inn.

 Christmas Prelude, a festival of lights, music, food, and traditional evergreen decorations, occurs the first weekend of December.

How to get there: Take Exit 3, Kennebunk, from the Maine Turnpike. Turn left onto State Route 35 and follow signs through Kennebunk to Kennebunkport. Turn left at the traffic light, cross the drawbridge, and take the first right onto Ocean Avenue. Turn left at the fifth intersection off Ocean. The inn is in the second block on the left.

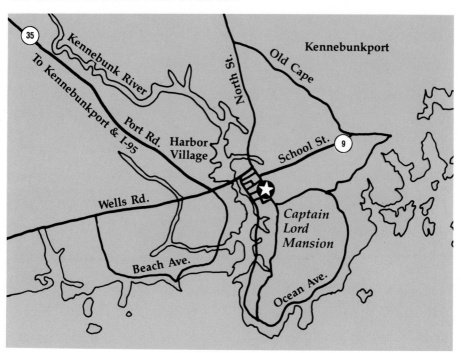

Captain Lord Mansion   ▲ **Phenix Inn**

Governor Calvert ▲   ▼ Admiral Fell Inn

45

HISTORIC INNS OF ANNAPOLIS

Annapolis harbor was once port of entry for goods and settlers heading for Baltimore, Washington and beyond. Today, Annapolis boasts many pre-Revolutionary houses, colonial mansions and small trade shops, stately Federal and Victorian-period homes, and the Historic Inns of Annapolis, five handsomely restored buildings in the center of the the Historic District.

The hub of the Historic Inns is the Maryland Inn. Over 200 years ago it hosted delegates to the Continental Congress. Today, visitors to Annapolis still enjoy the style and service of this Revolutionary period inn, with its Victorian additions, forty-four well-appointed guest rooms, and balconies that overlook the harbor.

The Reynolds Tavern has welcomed travelers since 1747, and its site near the old city gates on West Street made it a convenient stop for colonial travelers coming to Annapolis by land. Today, it belongs to the National Trust for Historic Preservation. Many artifacts uncovered during restoration of the inn are on exhibit there. Four guest rooms, a garden, and the restored tavern again welcome travelers to Annapolis.

Governor Calvert House, overlooking the State Capitol and the Old Treasury Building, was once the home of an early Maryland governor. Its restoration and conversion features a cleverly designed atrium between the original 18th century building, with nine guest rooms, and a new addition housing forty-six guest rooms, several meeting rooms, and a ballroom.

Facing the State House and with a view of the governor's mansion is the Robert Johnson House. Created from a block of four colonial homes, the inn was entirely renovated behind its historic facade. Its thirty guest rooms are appointed with fine antiques and reproductions, and it features a seasonal terrace and wine bar.

The Victorian State House Inn, with nine guest rooms, is situated between State Circle and Main Street. It houses the Hampton House Restaurant, which features turn-of-the-century Austro-Hungarian cuisine and decor.

Historic Inns of Annapolis   800-533-INNS
16 Church Circle   In Maryland 800-247-INNS
Annapolis, MD 21401

 The Maryland Inn's Treaty of Paris Restaurant is open every night. The King's Wine Cellar offers private dining for small parties. Both the Maryland Inn and the Governor Calvert House offer banquet service. Reynolds Tavern recreates an early American atmosphere complete with staff dressed in colonial garb, and a menu of period and regional foods.

 In the Maryland Inn, the Drummer's Lot, a colonial pub, and the King of France Tavern, with nightly jazz and other music, serve a complete assortment of spirits and beverages.

 Entirely new inside, the Governor Calvert Conference Center is an integration of Colonial and Victorian-era residences overlooking the State House. The Maryland Inn also offers accommodations for small conference groups.

46

Annapolis, Maryland

Annapolis is a mecca for sailors and powerboaters using the harbor and Chesapeake Bay. Nearby marshes and coves provide excellent canoeing and kayaking. The charter ship Mystic Clipper sails from City Dock during summer and fall.

Walking tours may be arranged with Historic Annapolis, Inc., or Three Centuries Tours of Annapolis. Both groups offer complete conference planning services.

Annapolis and the upper bay area are rich in historic sites, folklife, early architecture, and displays of America's revolutionary heritage.

The Naval Academy and St. John's College, with many cultural and athletic events, are only a few blocks from the Historic Inns. The Maryland Hall for Creative Arts houses the Annapolis Symphony, Annapolis Ballet, and a large variety of arts programs, classes, and studios.

The city sponsors a Spring Festival and summertime Arts Festival at City Dock. The Sail and Powerboat shows are held each autumn. Anne Arundel County Fairgrounds present an annual County Fair and the Renaissance Festival. Nearby Sandy Point State Park is the locale of two special autumn events, the Maryland Seafood Festival and Chesapeake Appreciation Days.

How to get there: From US 50, take the Rowe Boulevard exit to a dead end at College Avenue. Turn right and continue around Church Circle to the Maryland Inn, on the corner with Main Street, to check into any of the inns.

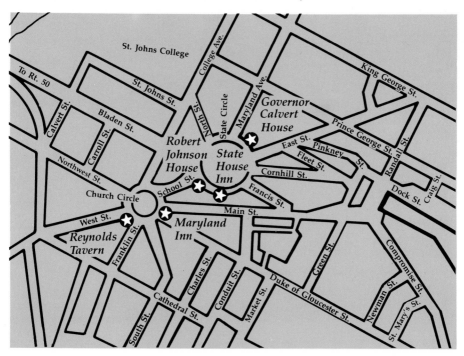

ADMIRAL FELL INN

The Admiral Fell Inn, located on the waterfront only minutes from Baltimore's Inner Harbor attractions and museums, consists of three connected historic buildings constructed between 1850 and 1910. Guest room windows provide a view of the harbor: tugboats guiding ships into port; yachts passing by on their way to the Inner Harbor.

The buildings have been completely renovated, and the inn has thirty-seven rooms and suites. Each guest room is unique in size and shape, and all are furnished with period antiques.

In the lobby, an oversize partners' desk serves as the reception desk, and a working fireplace graces the drawing room. An honor bar is set up in the library each evening. Guests are welcome to fix a drinks and take them to their rooms or to any of the sitting areas: a four-story atrium with plants and garden benches, the courtyard, the drawing room, the library.

Newspapers are delivered to guest rooms each morning, shoes are shined upon request, and complimentary van transportation in downtown Baltimore City is available for each guest.

Admiral Fell Inn   800-533-INNS
888 South Broadway   In Maryland 800-247-INNS
Baltimore, MD 21231

 Complimentary continental breakfast is served daily. Luncheon and dinner are served in the Admiral Fell Inn Pub and Restaurant. Catering arrangements can also be made.

 Meeting space is available for groups of up to fifty.

 Boat mooring is available across the street from the inn.

 The inn is located in a National Historic District. A walking tour may be made of Fell's Point. There are many historic sites and monuments in Baltimore.

 The inn is situated less than five minutes from the Johns Hopkins Hospital and Medical Schools complex. Goucher College, Notre Dame, Loyola, and Johns Hopkins University are also nearby.

Baltimore, Maryland

 Fell's Point has an abundance of small shops, offering an array of goods from maritime curiosities to classic Irish and Scottish fashions. The pavilions of Harborplace are also close by.

 Baltimore has many theatres and concert halls. The Morris Mechanic, Center Stage, Vagabond Theatre, Fell's Point Dinner Theatre, Harborlights Summer Concert Series, Lyric Opera House and Baltimore Symphony Orchestra are all a part of the city's theatrical diversity.

 Preakness Week surrounds the May running of the Preakness Stakes at Pimlico racetrack. The Ethnic Festival series culminates with the City Fair in September, and the Fell's Point Fun Festival is held every October.

How to get there: From Interstate 95, go north or downtown on Russell Street to Pratt Street. Turn right and continue east on Pratt Street around the Inner Harbor via Falls Avenue and Eastern Avenue to Broadway. Turn right and continue to the end of Broadway at Thames Street. The inn is on the right.

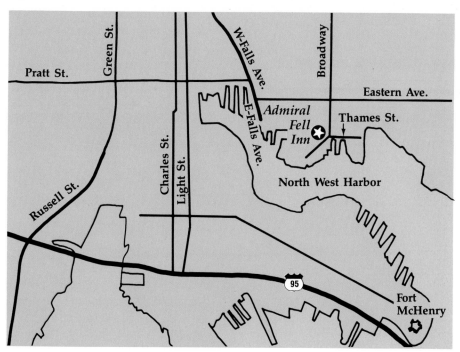

ANDOVER INN

Located on the campus of Phillips Andover Academy, the Andover Inn offers a relaxed atmosphere in a peaceful and undisturbed setting. The thirty-three guest rooms blend a nostalgic charm of things past with modern services and conveniences. All rooms have a view of garden, pond, or campus grounds.

The elegant dining room and lobby bar are well known for fine continental cuisine and extensive beverage selections. On Sunday evenings a special Rijsttafel is served in the dining room. This Indonesian extravaganza is unique in the area and very popular.

The Andover Inn attracts an interesting blend of guests: vacationers, business travelers, alumni and parents of Phillips Academy students, members of the academic community, and conference groups. All share an appreciation of the inn as more than just a place to stay, but as a special experience.

Andover Inn   800-533-INNS
Chapel Avenue   In Maryland 800-247-INNS
Andover, MA 01810

A la carte breakfast is served on weekdays and a buffet breakfast on weekends. Lunch is served daily, excluding weekends, and dinner is served nightly. On Sundays a buffet brunch is served and in the evening an Indonesian Rijsttafel. The inn also can serve conference and function meals.

The inn has a full-service bar and lounge. The wine list is extensive, complementing the dining room menu.

The function room can seat up to sixty.

The inn is thirty minutes away from the many Boston and area historic sites.

Andover, Massachusetts

 Phillips Academy, a well-known coeducational boarding high school, adjoins the inn. Merrimack College is nearby. Many cultural events throughout the school year are open to the public.

 Andover Center is within walking distance. Many indoor malls are nearby.

 Lawrence Airport, fifteen minutes away, has aviation fuel and rental cars available.

How to get there: Just south of Interstate 495, leave Interstate 93 at Exit 41, and take State Route 125 northeast two miles to State Route 28. Exit to go north on 28 about five miles to Phillips Academy. The Andover Inn is to the right, facing the north edge of the campus.

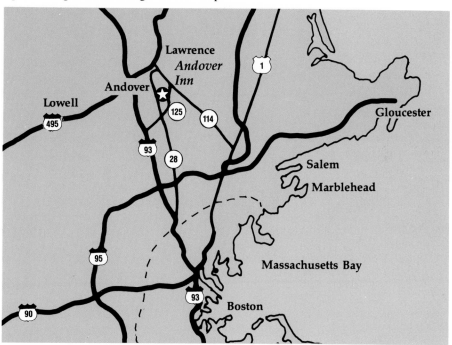

Andover Inn ▲   ▼ Yankee Clipper Inn

Dan'l Webster Inn ⬍

YANKEE CLIPPER INN

The Yankee Clipper Inn was once an ocean-front estate in a residental area near the remarkably picturesque artists' colony of Rockport, on Cape Ann. The inn consists of three converted estate buildings on extensive grounds, with twenty-eight guest rooms. The main building is a mansion with antique furnishings, canopy beds, glass-enclosed porches, and private and public sun decks.

The dining room is right on the water, and buffet luncheons are served on the outside terrace in July and August. The Quarterdeck offers views through large picture windows directly overlooking the ocean.

The more distant Bulfinch house was designed by and is named for the famous early American architect who also designed the Massachusetts State House on Boston's Beacon Hill. Here guests may find all the comforts of home in a classic early 19th century New England house of clipper ship days.

Yankee Clipper Inn   Inn 800-533-INNS
Box 2399   In Maryland 800-247-INNS
96 Granite Street
Rockport, MA 01966

 Full breakfast and dinner are served in the oceanfront dining room mid-May to mid-October. In winter, a generous complimentary continental breakfast is offered.

 Rockport is a dry town. Guests must bring their own beer, wine, or liquor. Setups are available in the dining room.

 Conference facilities are available for groups of up to twenty-five. Audiovisual equipment is also available.

 Inn guests may play on the Rockport Country Club's nine-hole golf course.

 The inn provides tours of Gloucester harbor in the inn's own boat, in season. In town, whale-watching boat trips with a local naturalist are available.

 Deep-sea fishing is a very popular sport, on boats sailing from Rockport and Gloucester harbors.

Rockport, Massachusetts

 An outdoor, heated saltwater swimming pool is in the garden. Ocean beach swimming is nearby.

 The inn is within one hour of most of the important historic sites in the Boston area, including Salem, Lexington, and Concord.

 Rockport is celebrated for art galleries featuring local artists, handicraft shops, and gift and antique shops.

 The Rockport Chamber Music Festival is held during the first three weeks of June.

How to get there: Take Interstate 95 northeast to State Route 128 and continue northeast on 128 all the way to Cape Ann, where it ends at the first set of traffic lights. Turn left onto State Route 127. Go four miles to a sharp left toward Pigeon Cove. One and a half miles further along this road is the inn.

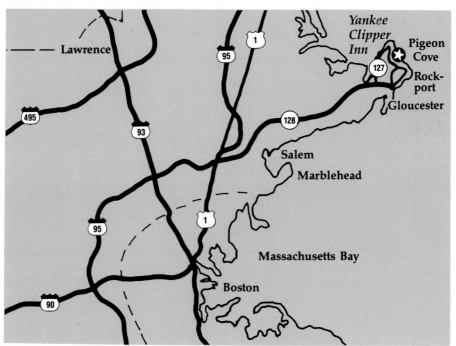

DAN'L WEBSTER INN

The original building of Dan'l Webster Inn was erected in 1692 as a parsonage. In 1750 it became the Fessendon Tavern, one of the first and most famous taverns in Colonial America. During the Revolution it served as patriot headquarters.

After that war, the tavern became a frequent stop for visitors to Cape Cod. Henry David Thoreau, Grover Cleveland, Helen Keller, actor Joseph Jefferson, and Daniel Webster himself all enjoyed the cape for hunting, fishing, or simply relaxing.

The inn is situated on quiet, historic Main Street of Sandwich village. A drive along the old King's Highway through coastal villages reveals many antique shops, galleries, spectacular views of the sand dunes at Sandy Neck and the National Seashore, and other opportunities for leisurely exploration.

The inn offers forty-two guest rooms with colonial appointments and modern conveniences. Some rooms have canopy beds, some have Hitchcock furniture, and others have private balconies overlooking well-kept flower gardens.

The Dan'l Webster Suite, on top of the main building, has a living room, double whirlpool bath with skylight, and a view of the Great Marsh. In Fessendon House, a restored sea-captain's home, there are two-room suites with whirlpool baths and living rooms with fireplaces.

The inn is convenient to get to from all major cities, and Boston is an hour away.

Dan'l Webster Inn
149 Main Street
Sandwich, MA 02563

800-533-INNS
In Maryland 800-247-INNS

 The award-winning restaurant with three dining rooms serves fresh local seafood and continental cuisine, and is open every day from 8 a.m. to 10 p.m.

 The Tavern and lounge have full bar service, and offer entertainment most nights.

 Conference groups up to fifty can be accommodated in meeting rooms fully equipped with audiovisual aids.

 Nearby for golf are Holly Ridge (par three), Round Hill Country Club, and Quashnet Valley.

 Town tennis courts with lights are a mile away.

 An outdoor swimming pool is open in season, and the cape is surrounded by ocean beaches.

Sandwich, Massachusetts

 Saltwater sport fishing is available from nearly all local harbors.

 Whale-watch cruises depart from Barnstable Harbor, twenty minutes from the inn.

 Sandwich was founded in 1642. Many old homes flank historic Old King's Highway. The Doll Museum, the famous Sandwich Glass Museum, Thornton Burgess Museum, and Heritage Plantation are all within two miles of the inn.

 Many antique and other specialty shops are within walking distance.

 Summer stock theatre is alive on Cape Cod all summer.

 The Barnstable County Fair runs for a week in late July.

How to get there: At Sagamore Bridge cross Cape Cod Canal and exit from State Route 6 at Exit 2. Turn left and follow State Route 130 for two miles. As a pond and grist mill appear on the left, bear right at the fork. The inn is 300 yards ahead on the left.

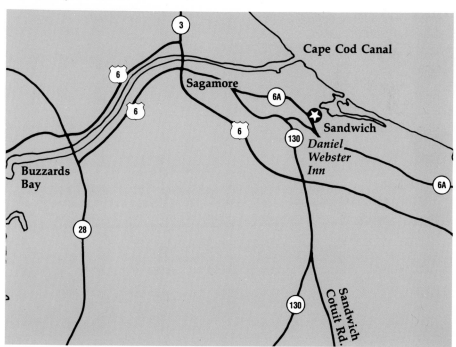

THE BURN

One of Natchez' historic homes, The Burn was built in 1832. During the Civil War, it was used first as Union headquarters and later as a Union hospital. The facade is pure Greek revival. The front portico is supported by large Doric columns, and the paneled doorway is framed in side lights of early glass.

Horses once trod through the entrance hall, where a collection of irreplaceable antique furniture now resides. The gas lights of the chandeliers add a romantic glow to the Empire dining room, which is appointed with matching Regency servers and Old Paris china. Aubusson carpets and fine Belgian fabrics adorn the six bedrooms in the main house and in an original dependency, still in use on the grounds.

Arriving guests are treated to a tour of the mansion.

The Burn
712 North Union Street
Natchez, MS 39120

800-533-INNS
In Maryland 800-247-INNS

 A seated plantation breakfast is complimentary. Special Magnolia seated dinner parties, lunches, and picnics may be arranged for groups of twenty or more.

 Golf and tennis are available in the city park a half mile away.

 A private pool is situated in the inn gardens.

 Natchez celebrates its history all year round, with the Natchez Trace, paddlewheel riverboats on the Mississippi River, and more than five hundred antebellum buildings, including many elegant mansions open for visitors.

 Antique shops and local craft shops are located in the restored Historic Downtown District.

Natchez, Mississippi

 Entertainment throughout the year includes the Confederate Pageant, the Mississippi Medicine Show in the Natchez Little Theatre Playhouse, and Moonlight and Magnolias dinner theatre in the Carriage House.

 The annual House Pilgrimages take place in spring and fall, complete with pagentry and authentic dress reminiscent of planter aristocracy. Victorian-style celebrations highlight the Christmas season in Natchez.

 Hardy-Anders Field, seven miles northeast of town, has aviation fuel and rental cars.

How to get there: Follow US 61, business route, to Union Street, one-way north. The Burn is on the left, just beyond Bee Street.

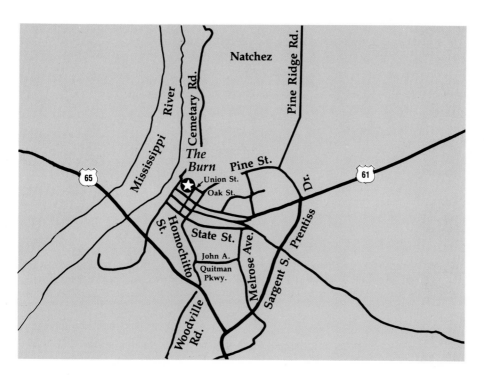

MONMOUTH PLANTATION

Built in 1818, this twenty-six-acre antebellum plantation was purchased in 1826 by General John Quitman for his bride, Eliza. The Quitman family lived there until 1905. As part of the 1978 restoration, many family artifacts and original furnishings were located and returned, including a ceremonial sword given the general by President Polk.

The plantation has thirteen guest rooms, five in the mansion, four in the original kitchen building, and four in the garden area. Each room is furnished with period antiques, yet has all the modern conveniences.

Arriving guests are treated to a tour of the house. The inn and its Civil War museum are listed on the National Register of Historic Places.

Monmouth Plantation
P.O. Box 1736
Natchez, MS 39120

800-533-INNS
In Maryland 800-247-INNS

 A full Southern breakfast is complimentary.

 Golf and tennis are available in the city park a half mile away.

 Guests may fish from Monmouth's own stocked pond on the grounds.

 Vineyard and winery tours are available.

 Natchez celebrates its history all year round, with the Natchez Trace, paddlewheel riverboats on the Mississippi River, and more than five hundred antebellum buildings, including many elegant mansions open for visitors.

 Antique shops and local craft shops are located in the restored Historic Downtown District.

Natchez, Mississippi

 Entertainment throughout the year includes the Confederate Pageant, the Mississippi Medicine Show in the Natchez Little Theatre Playhouse, and Moonlight and Magnolias dinner theatre in the Carriage House.

 The annual House Pilgrimages take place in spring and fall, complete with pagentry and authentic dress reminiscent of planter aristocracy. Victorian-style celebrations highlight the Christmas season in Natchez.

 Hardy-Anders Field, seven miles northeast of town, has aviation fuel and rental cars.

How to get there: Turn off US 61, Sargent S. Prentiss Drive, north onto Melrose Avenue. Turn left at John A. Quitman Parkway, and left again into the Monmouth driveway.

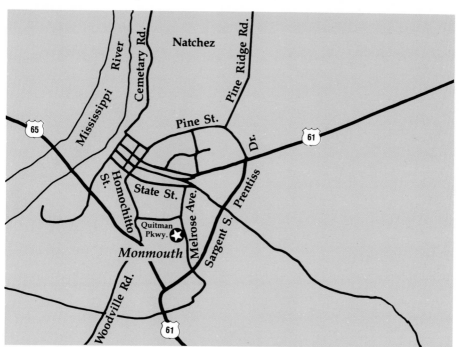

Monmouth Plantation   ▼ **Anchuca**

Cedar Grove Mansion

ANCHUCA

Anchuca is the ancient Indian word for "happy home." The inn named Anchuca, recently restored and placed on the National Register of Historic Places, rises above brick paved streets in the heart of historic Vicksburg.

The house was originally built about 1830 as a one-floor wood building. It later received a Greek revival facade, with part of the wood structure shaved off to accommodate the elaborate "front." Jefferson Davis is reported to have made a speech from the balcony above the main entrance.

About 1840 the slave quarters, made of century-old brick, were added to the rear of the house. In 1900 a cottage was built on the property. The cottage and slave quarters have been transformed into nine guest rooms furnished with period antiques and gas-burning chandeliers.

Arriving guests are treated to a mint julip and tour of the mansion.

Anchuca
1010 First East Street
Vicksburg, MS 39180

800-533-INNS
In Maryland 800-247-INNS

 A complimentary breakfast is served in the formal dining room. There are excellent restaurants close by for other meals.

 A complimentary glass of wine or a mint julip is offered to each guest.

 Guests may swim in the inn's private pool and relax in the whirlpool bath in the pool cabana.

 The battle of Vicksburg is commemorated in the National Military Park. Daily cruises on the Spirit of Vicksburg riverboat feature a descriptive narrative of the Seige of Vicksburg. There are also many historic homes and museums to explore.

Vicksburg, Mississippi

 Antique shops and modern boutiques are located nearby.

 The annual melodrama "Gold in the Hills," approaching its 50th season, is performed during the spring and summer at the Parkside Theatre. The local theatre has productions throughout the year with a Vicksburg cast.

 Vicksburg Municipal Airport, eight miles soutwest of the city, has aviation fuel and rental cars.

How to get there: Off Interstate 20, take Exit 1C onto Halls Ferry Road, and go north until it becomes Cherry Street, which then becomes Fort Hill Drive. Turn right at First East Street for the inn.

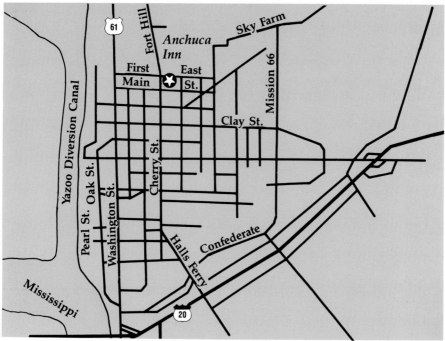

CEDAR GROVE MANSION

Cedar Grove Mansion was built between 1840 and 1858 by wealthy businessman John Klein as a wedding gift for his bride, Elizabeth. Many notables visited Cedar Grove, including Jefferson Davis, who danced in the ballroom, and U. S. Grant, who slept in the Mallard bed in the master bedroom.

Today a restored Cedar Grove is said to "begin the grand parade of mansions from Vicksburg to New Orleans." Many of the original furnishings remain, including imported gold-leaf mirrors from Paris, marble mantels from Italy, and the Mallard bed and master bedroom, which is now a guestroom. Also remaining is a grim reminder of the Civil War, a Union cannonball lodged in the wall of the parlor hall.

Guests are accommodated in eighteen antebellum-style rooms in the mansion, in "Little Tara," a mini-mansion, and in a poolside guesthouse in the courtyard. Surrounding the inn are four acres of gardens with gazebos, fountains, and fish ponds.

Cedar Grove is listed on the National Register of Historic Places.

Cedar Grove Mansion   800-533-INNS
2200 Oak Street   In Maryland 800-247-INNS
Vicksburg, MS 39180

 A complimentary full breakfast is served by butlers in the dining room. Exellent restaurants are close by for other meals.

 A complimentary mint julip made from the inn's own receipe, white wine, or a soft drink are offered to guests.

 Guests may swim in the inn pool in the mansion courtyard. A whirlpool bath is on the grounds.

 Guides are available for tours of historic Vicksburg town. Daily riverboat cruises feature a narrative of the Seige of Vicksburg.

 Nearby is a restored downtown area with many boutiques and shops.

Vicksburg, Mississippi

 The annual melodrama "Gold in the Hills," approaching its 50th season, is performed during the spring and summer at the Parkside Theatre.

 An annual pilgrimage of historic homes, with Cedar Grove as a headliner, is made in late March.

 Vicksburg Municipal Airport, eight miles soutwest of the city, has aviation fuel and rental cars.

How to get there: From Interstate 20, take Exit 1A, Washington Street. Go north on Washington for two and a half miles and turn left on Klein Street. The mansion is on the corner of Klein and Oak Street.

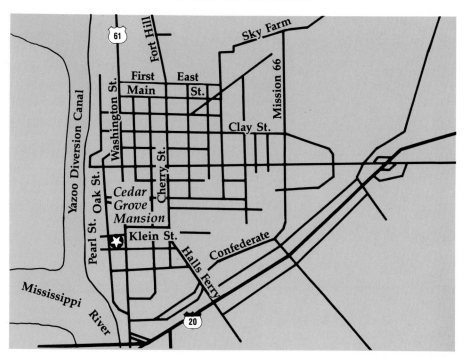

KONA MANSION INN

The main building of Kona Mansion Inn was built in 1900 as a summer home by Boston retailing executive Herbert Dumeresq. It was the centerpiece of a grand estate he assembled by buying several local farms during the 1890s. He called his retreat Kona Farm, appropriating an old Indian name for the area.

The owner wanted his house to be substantial, comfortable, and self-sustaining. The lower walls are solid stone. The upper walls, made of wood, are insulated with coastal seaweed. The house has eight fireplaces, installed to burn oak logs from trees on the estate.

By 1971, the estate had been gradually whittled down to its present one hundred and thirty acres. The big house had become the present inn, with fourteen guest rooms, and has been preserved as an active monument to America's vanished age of elegance.

Kona Mansion Inn
P.O. Box 458
Center Harbor, NH 03226

800-533-INNS
In Maryland 800-247-INNS

 Breakfast and dinner are served through October. Box lunches are available for guests. Complete catering is available for conferences and receptions.

 Complete bar service is offered in the Sunset Lounge and in the dining room.

 Conference groups up to thirty-five can be accommodated overnight and in the meeting room.

 A private par-three golf course overlooks the lake. Clubs may be rented.

 Twin tennis courts with an all-weather surface are on the grounds.

Center Harbor, New Hampshire

 The mansion has a private sandy beach on the lake.

 Guests may fish in the lake from the pier or from the inn's rowboats. Nearby marinas have powerboats for rent.

 Many antique and auction houses are nearby. Brand-name factory outlet stores are in North Conway and Laconia.

 The Inn will pick up private-plane passengers at Moultonboro airport.

How to get there: Leave Interstate 93 at Exit 23 and follow State Route 104 to Meredith. Turn right at the traffic light in Meredith onto State Route 25. Go eight miles and turn right onto Moultonborough Neck Road, and follow the Kona Mansion signs to the inn.

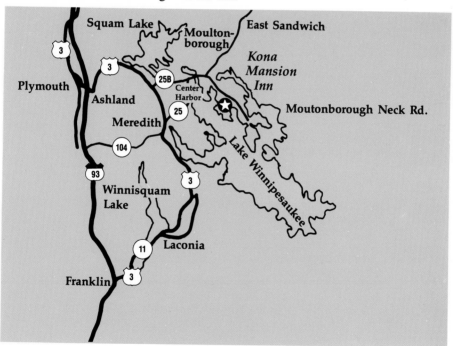

INN AT THORN HILL

Offering spectacular mountain views in every direction, including Mount Washington and the entire Presidential range, the Inn at Thorn Hill is nestled in the heart of the White Mountains in the quaint village of Jackson. Guests approach through a covered bridge, and discover the inn situated on a quiet country road surrounded by six landscaped acres.

The inn was designed and built by Stanford White, the well-known New York architect and socialite. The main building and carriage house have been carefully restored, and furnished in turn-of-the-century style.

Guests may relax on the porch in New England rocking chairs, or snuggle by the fireplace in the expansive living room. The nineteen antique-filled guest rooms offer a welcome retreat after a few pleasant hours in the pub or in the dining room, noted for its elegant candlelit dinners.

Inn at Thorn Hill   800-533-INNS
Jackson Village, NH 03846   In Maryland 800-247-INNS

Breakfast and dinner are served daily and complimentary snacks are offered in the lounge. Complete dining service is provided for conference groups.

Full bar service is available, including a select wine list.

An eighteen-hole PGA golf course with a full-service pro shop is within walking distance of the inn.

Tennis and raquetball, both indoor and outdoor, are available nearby.

For swimming, an Olympic-sized pool and a spring-fed duckpond are on the grounds.

Four downhill ski areas are within ten minutes of the inn, and one hundred and forty kilometres of groomed cross-country trails pass right by the inn.

A riding stable is within walking distance of the inn.

70

Jackson Village, New Hampshire

 Many factory outlet stores, antique shops, and craft shops may be found in Jackson Village and nearby Conway.

 Plays and concerts are regular events during the season in Jackson Village and Conway.

 New England is well-known for its country fairs. The largest in the region is held every year in Fryeburg, Maine, a half hour drive from the inn. Other festivals include Concerts in the Park, Arts Jubilee, Winterfest, and Jumping in the Clouds.

How to get there: Leave Interstate 93 at Exit 24 and go east to Ashland. Follow US 3 and State Route 25 and 25B east to Center Harbor. Continue on 25 to Whittier. Turn left on State Route 113 and continue to State Route 16. Turn left and follow State Route 16 to Jackson.

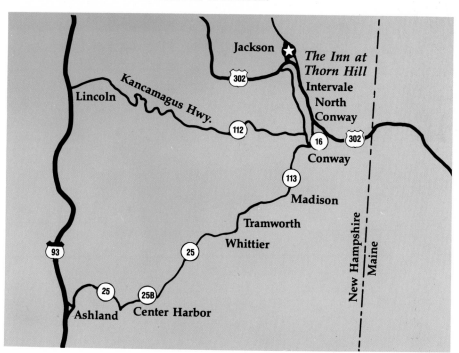

Kona Mansion Inn ▼   ▲ Mainstay Inn

Mainstay Inn ▲　　　　　▼ **Inn at Thorn Hill**

73

MAINSTAY INN

In 1872 two wealthy gamblers built an elegant, exclusive clubhouse in Cape May where they and their friends could pursue gambling and other gentlemanly amusements.

The result was a grand villa with fourteen-foot ceilings, ornate plaster mouldings, elaborate chandeliers, a sweeping veranda, and a cupola. Twelve-foot-high mirrors, marble-topped sideboards, and graceful loveseats were among the richly ornamented furnishings.

Today this beautiful building is a bed and breakfast inn in the heart of historic Cape May. Except for a few concessions to 20th century tastes, the inn is much the same as it was one hundred years ago.

Most of the twelve rooms are large. Some of the best rooms are in the Cottage, an 1870s summer house adjacent to the inn. All rooms are furnished entirely with Victorian antiques, many of which are original to the house.

Mainstay Inn
635 Columbia Avenue
Cape May, NJ 08204

800-533-INNS
In Maryland 800-247-INNS

 A family-style breakfast is served in the dining room or on the veranda. Homemade treats are featured at tea, open to the public. Numerous small gourmet restaurants are nearby.

 Several eighteen-hole golf courses are within fifteen miles of the inn.

 The Cape May Tennis Club, located six blocks from the inn, welcomes the public to play on clay and hard surface courts.

 The inn provides passes for local ocean beaches. Ocean temperatures are about seventy-five degrees in July and August.

 Cape May offers excellent jogging, bicycling, and hiking along the beach. Nature and hiking trails may be found in the state park two miles from the inn.

 Launching facilities for privately owned boats are near the inn. Excursion boats, both power and sail, operate throughout the season.

 Hidden Valley Ranch offers horseback riding on beach and dune trails, and holds competitive events at various times of the year.

Cape May, New Jersey

 Cape May is a National Historic Landmark town, and has the greatest concentration of Victorian structures in America.

 Walking and trolley tours are offered, and many homes are open to the public on a regular basis.

 Cape May's outdoor shopping mall features an array of cafes, art galleries, and specialty shops.

 Summer stock is presented in an open air setting in July and August at the Physick Estate, and concerts are held in the bandstand or in the convention hall on a regular basis.

How to get there: The Garden State Parkway terminates in Cape May and becomes Lafayette Street. Turn left at the first light after the canal bridge onto Madison Avenue. Go three blocks, then turn right onto Columbia Avenue. The inn is three blocks down Columbia, on the corner to the right.

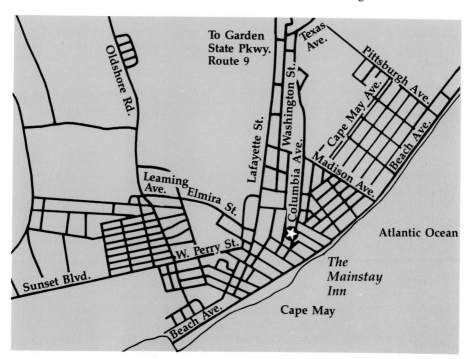

THE LODGE AT CLOUDCROFT

The historic Lodge, a Southwest railroad mountain resort, is situated 9,200 feet high on the southern tip of the Rocky Mountains, in Lincoln National Forest.

The all-season inn has hosted hundreds of prominent people since 1899, and serves as a destination for visitors to the many famous nearby desert attractions such as Carlsbad Caverns and White Sands National Monument.

It is also said to be the haunt of a beautiful red-haired ghost named Rebecca, who legend says disappeared after her lumberjack lover found her in the arms of another.

Bavarian in style with a Victorian flavor, the recently restored Lodge has forty-seven guest rooms and many public rooms, parlors, dining rooms, and lounges, all filled with antiques.

Among its many attractions is a five-story copper tower with a seventy-five-mile panoramic view of pine forests to white-sand deserts.

The Lodge   800-533-INNS
P.O. Box 497   In Maryland 800-247-INNS
Cloudcroft, NM 88317

 Meals are served three times daily in fireside, mountain view, and outdoor dining areas. The cuisine features European specialties, prime meats, fresh seafood, and flambe and tableside preparation.

 Full bar service is offered daily in Rebecca's Lounge, the Red Dog Saloon, and the Nineteenth Hole golf bar.

 Six on-premises meeting and banquet rooms can accommodate groups of up to 100. Audiovisual equipment is available.

 The Lodge has its own dramatically scenic eighteeen-hole golf course, par 68 and 4818 yards.

 A full range of winter sports is available: downhill skiing at the Cloudcroft Ski Area, cross-country skiing on the golf course and forest service trails, snowmobiling, four-wheeling, sledding, and ice skating.

Cloudcraft, New Mexico

 A spa, sauna, and heated swimming pool overlooking the golf course offer year-round swimming.

 Nearly all summer activities are available locally, including horseback riding, trail riding, biking, hunting, hiking, and camping.

 Numerous scenic, historic, natural and sports attractions are a half hour to a two and a half hour drive, including Carlsbad Caverns, White Sands National Monument, International Space Hall of Fame, Mescalero Apache Reservation and Ruidoso resort, Smoky the Bear Museum, and Juarez, Mexico.

 Country craft gifts are available at The Lodge Mercantile. Jewelry and regional art are sold in The Lodge goldsmith's shop. Many craft shops are located in Cloudcroft.

How to get there: From US 54, three miles north of Alamogordo, take US 82 east sixteen miles to Cloudcroft. Near the center of town, watch for the Lodge sign on the right.

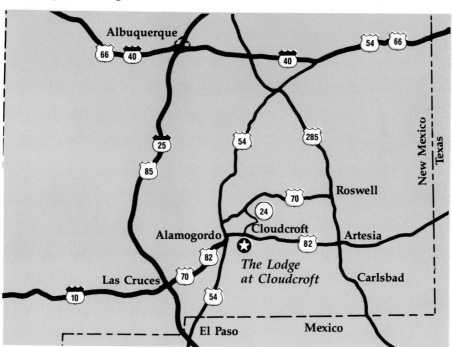

PLAZA HOTEL

In 1882 the Plaza Hotel was built in the busy commercial center of Las Vegas, in the young New Mexico territory. From 1886 to 1900 business was brisk, and many notorious outlaws and infamous characters of the Old West stayed at the Plaza, including Doc Holiday and Big Nose Kate, Vicente Silva, and Billy the Kid.

By 1913, the era of silent films brought another wave of popularity to Las Vegas and the Plaza, and the hotel became a film and studio headquarters. Later, many scenes from the popular Tom Mix series were filmed in and around Las Vegas, incorporating shots of the Plaza Hotel in several episodes.

In 1982, the hotel was carefully restored to its former splendor. Architectural documentation and historical and cultural studies were done to assure the accuracy of the project.

The hotel, with thirty-eight rooms and suites, is now on the National Register of Historic Places.

Plaza Hotel   800-533-INNS
230 Old Town Plaza   In Maryland 800-247-INNS
Las Vegas, NM 87701

 A full-service restaurant in the hotel serves all meals. Cuisine is New Mexican. Complete dining service for meetings and groups is available.

 Full bar service in the hotel and table service in the dining room are available.

 Groups of up to forty can be accommodated in suites, in the meeting room, or in the conservatory.

 Golf is available in a spectacular mountain meadow setting at the Pendaries Golf Club.

 Nearby Santa Fe National Forest has cross-country ski trails, and Las Vegas has one of the few outdoor skating ponds in the Southwest.

 The area is noted for excellent trout fishing. Both stream and lake fishing are available within fifteen miles of town.

Las Vegas, New Mexico

 Nature tours can be arranged to Lake McAllister waterfowl area, host to a variety of migratory birds.

 Las Vegas has more than 1300 structures listed in the National Register of Historic Places. Within thirty miles of town are Fort Union National Monument and Pecos National Monument.

 New Mexico Highlands University is located in Las Vegas. Nearby at historic Montezuma Hot Springs is the Armand Hammer United World College.

 Las Vegas Municipal Airport has aviation fuel and rental cars available.

How to get there: Leave Interstate 25 at Exit 345 and follow the Plaza signs west through town.

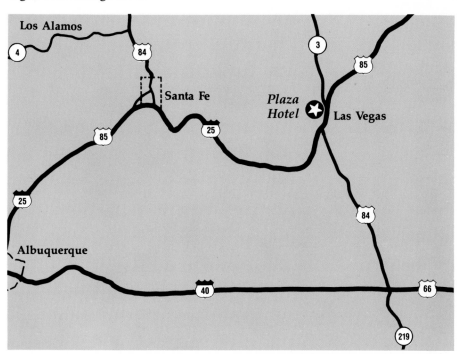

TAOS INN

Taos is a world-famous artists colony, whose history is linked to the Taos Inn. The inn restaurant, Doc Martin's, was the home and office of the town's first physician, T. Paul Martin. In 1912 he and two artist friends gathered in his dining room to develop the idea leading to the formation of the Taos Society of Artists.

After Martin's death in 1936, his widow bought the Tarleton house next door, now the Adobe Bar, and enclosed the plaza to create the lobby of the Hotel Martin. The fountain in the center of the lobby was the old town well. Later owners changed the name to Taos Inn and added the neon Thunderbird sign, the oldest in Taos.

In 1981 and 1982 the inn, whose buildings date from the 1800s, was restored. The forty guest rooms feature pueblo-style fireplaces designed by a noted local sculptor. Each room is furnished with antiques, hand-loomed Indian bedspreads, and handcrafted furniture.

An outstanding example of Santa Fe and pueblo revival styles of architecture, the inn is listed on the National and State Registers of Historic Places.

Taos Inn   800-533-INNS
P.O. Drawer N   In Maryland 800-247-INNS
Taos, NM 87571

Doc Martin's restaurant features native specialties and homemade desserts. Three meals are served daily.

The Adobe bar offers full bar service, and is a popular gathering spot for local artists and writers.

Taos Ski Valley is a world-famous ski area and school.

The inn has a heated pool for swimming in the summer.

The inn has a whirlpool bath on premises and a full-facility spa nearby, which includes tennis and racquetball courts, with lessons available.

Tours of artists' studios are part of the inn's meet-the-artists series each fall and spring. Walking tours of historic Taos leave the inn each morning at 11:00.

Taos, New Mexico

 The inn is located in the center of an historic district and is in easy walking distance of such historic sites as the Fechin Institute and Kit Carson's home.

 Only a minute's walk from the inn's front door are the famous shops and galleries of Taos.

 The inn is next door to the Taos Community Auditorium and the Stables Art Center, where many performing and visual arts events take place year round.

 The Taos Spring Arts Celebration, with various daily events, runs from May 25 through June 21. The Fall Arts Festival is October 1 through 7. The Balloon Festival is in October.

How to get there: Follow State Route 3, North Pueblo Road, into the center of town. The inn is on this road, just north of Taos Plaza.

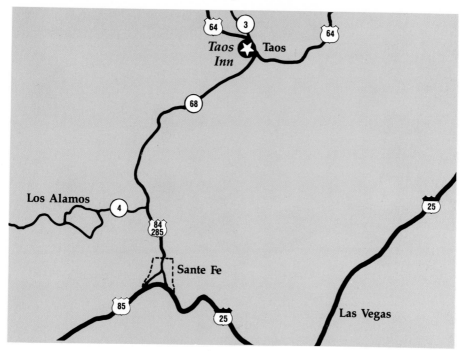

Taos Inn ⬍

82

Gregory House 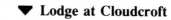 **Lodge at Cloudcroft**

TROUTBECK

Troutbeck estate was once the home of poet-naturalist Myron Benton, whose friends John Burroughs, Ralph Waldo Emerson, and Henry David Thoreau visited him there. Later a gathering place for the literati and liberals of the 1920s, Troutbeck is only two hours from midtown New York City.

Surrounded by landscaped gardens, streams, lakes, and the woods of the Berkshires, the present English-style manor house is approached through towering sycamore trees planted in 1835, a scene that Sinclair Lewis once described as "a cathedral of trees."

Troutbeck now hosts corporate conference groups during the week and country escapes for weekend guests. The thirty-one guest rooms are quiet retreats. The living room, with pleasing color and print, is highlighted by beamed ceilings, leaded windows, and a crackling fireplace. Troutbeck has 12,000 books in its library and many comfortable nooks and wing chairs where guests can settle down to read.

Among Troutbeck's attractions are the winter garden dining room, which serves imaginative and acclaimed cuisine. The conference room has massive beams, a stone fireplace, and many doors and windows opening onto a patio and deck. A few steps from the main house is the Century Farmhouse, which has a restored two-hundred-and-forty-year-old wing.

Troutbeck
Leedsville Road
Amenia, NY 12501

800-553-INNS
In Maryland 800-247-INNS

 Troutbeck serves all meals, and offers an open bar for corporate and weekend guests.

 Conference groups up to forty are accommodated in the conference room, which is fully equipped with audiovisual aids. Only one corporate group is booked at a time, so the entire house is available.

 There are two nine-hole golf courses within fifteen minutes of Troutbeck and an eighteen-hole course a half hour away.

 Two all-weather tennis courts are on the grounds.

 Troutbeck is near Catamount and Butternut, major ski areas.

Amenia, New York

 Trout fishing is available in streams on the inn grounds. In the lake are small-mouth bass.

 Swimming may be enjoyed in indoor and outdoor pools.

 One poolhouse has a sauna and exercise room.

 Stables with indoor and outdoor rings and riding trails are a fifteen-minute drive away.

 Dutchess County airport, with aviation fuel and rental cars, is thirty minutes away. A helipad is just two minutes away.

How to get there: Take Interstate 684 north to Brewster, where it narrows to two lanes and becomes State Route 22. In Amenia turn right at the light onto State Route 343 and go two and a half miles to the Troutbeck sign on the right.

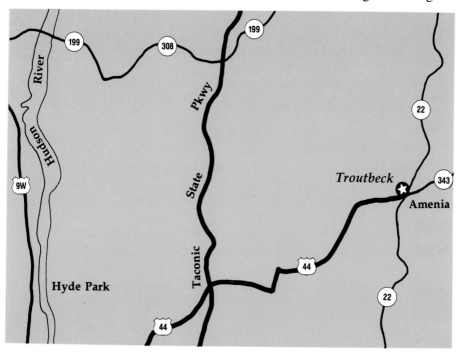

GREGORY HOUSE

In the long and colorful history of Rensselaer County in upstate New York, the names Hudson, Van Rensselaer, and Vanderheyden were joined by lesser known but equally significant contributors to early development. The Averill family gave its name to Averill Park, and in the early 1800s there were at least seven Gregory families prominent in local affairs.

What is known affectionately in the village as "the old Gregory house" was built by Elias Gregory about 1830 as a private home. The architectural style of the building is colonial, with several complementary additions built over the years to accommodate larger Gregory families.

In the 1960s the house passed on to other owners, and was later converted to a small, intimate restaurant. In 1984, the building was enlarged again to accommodate overnight guests. The inn now features a large common room with a fireplace for relaxing and socializing, and twelve comfortably furnished guest rooms.

Gregory House
P.O. Box 401
Averill Park, N.Y. 12018

800-553-INNS
In Maryland 800-247-INNS

 A complimentary continental breakfast is served to guests. Four candlelit dining rooms serve dinner each night except Monday.

 Full bar service is available in the common room and in the dining rooms.

 Sailing and windsurfing are available, including instruction, on Crystal Lake near the inn.

 Swimming is available in the inn pool and at Crystal Lake.

 Free, daily guided tours of the Empire State Plaza, the New York State Museum, and the state capitol building are available in Albany, fifteen minutes from the inn.

Averill Park, New York

 Cherry Hill, a home built by Philip Van Rensselaer in 1787, and Schuyler Mansion, home of Revolutionary War general Philip Schuyler, are nearby.

 Rensselaer Polytechnic Institute, founded in 1824, and Emma Willard School, the oldest school for women in the nation, are in nearby Troy.

 Empire State Institute for the Performing Arts and the Capital Repertory Company are in Albany. Mac-Hayden Summer Theatre in Chatham, the acoustically acclaimed Music Hall in Troy, and the theatre at Proctors in Schenectady offer entertainment throughout the year.

How to get there: From Interstate 90 take Exit 7, the first exit east of the Hudson River, and turn left onto Washington Avenue. Continue on Washington across US 4, and take State Route 43 seven and a half miles to Averill Park. Gregory House is on the left.

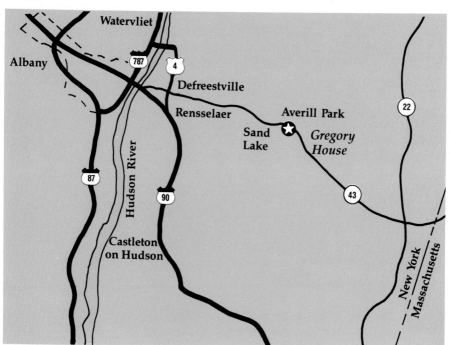

GENEVA ON THE LAKE

The Geneva on the Lake villa was built between 1910 and 1914 by industrialist Byron Nestor. It is a faithful replica, on a smaller scale, of the imposing and grand Lancellotti Villa in the Alban Hills outside Rome, Italy.

In the late 1940s the estate was donated by the Nestor family to the Catholic Church. It was a Capuchin monastery until 1981, when it was bought and converted into an inn and conference center.

The ten-acre estate with its formal gardens and woodland paths is situated on a bluff overlooking Seneca Lake, and has its own boat landing. The villa has twenty-nine suites, with marble fireplaces, woodwork carved in classical motifs, and gilt-coffered ceilings done in Italian Renaissance style.

An architectural and landscaping ensemble of historic merit, the inn has been placed on the National Register of Historic Places.

Geneva on the Lake
1001 Lochland Road
Geneva, NY 14456

800-553-INNS
In Maryland 800-247-INNS

 Complimentary continental breakfast and Sunday night buffet are served on a regular basis. Complete dining service is provided for conference groups. Five excellent restaurants are within a half mile.

 Conference groups up to thirty-five are accommodated in the meeting room, which is fully equipped with audiovisual aids. Groups up to ten can be accommodated in large suites.

 Golf is available at the Seneca Lake Country Club.

 Sailing and windsurfing are available, including instruction, at the inn's boat landing.

 Downhill and cross-country skiing are a short drive from the inn.

 Swimming may be enjoyed in the inn's seventy-foot pool, or in Seneca Lake.

Geneva, New York

 For fishing, outboard motor boats, guides and equipment are available at the inn boat landing.

 Tours of wineries in the Finger Lakes Region are a regular activity.

 Hobart College and William Smith College are in Geneva, and offer an assortment of academic events in session.

 Interesting visits may be made to Geneva's own historic district and restored mansions.

How to get there: From Interstate 90, the New York State Thruway, take Exit 42 and go south on State Route 14 ten miles to Geneva. Continue through the intersection with State Route 20 in Geneva. The inn is a half mile further south on Route 14.

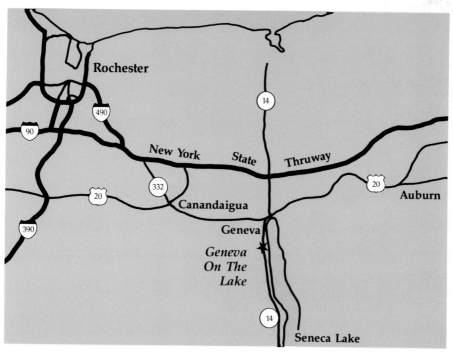

GENESEE COUNTRY INN

Genesee is an Iroquois word that means pleasant valley. In 1799, many Scots came to the valley to settle in the "dark, dense forest of evergreens" near what is now the historic hamlet of Mumford.

Nestled on six quiet and secluded acres in the village, the stone building that is the Genesee Country Inn was built in 1833 as a plaster mill. Later converted to manufacturing, it was sold in the early 1900s to a paper company and eventually became the residence of the plant manager.

Now the eighteen-room building has been completely restored and converted to a country inn. Spring Creek flows through the grounds, with ponds, waterfalls, and swimming ducks to please the eye. The ten guest rooms are decorated with hand stenciling and furnished with antiques, and each includes fresh flowers, handcrafted quilts, and a sitting area to relax in.

Genesee Country Inn   800-553-INNS
948 George Street   In Maryland 800-247-INNS
Mumford, NY 14511

 A complimentary full breakfast is served to guests. Complete dining service for conference groups can be arranged. Eight excellent restaurants are close by the inn.

 Conference groups of up to twenty-five are accommodated in the 1830s style meeting room overlooking the ponds.

 Golf may be played at nearby Caledonia Country Club, LeRoy Country Club, or Chili Country Club.

 Cross-country skiing, snowmobiling, and tobogganing are all available.

 Guests may fish, using their own equipment, in fully stocked trout streams on the inn grounds.

 The restored Genesee Country Village, spanning the late 1700s to the late 1800s, is less than a mile from the inn.

Mumford, New York

 The University of Rochester, the Eastman School of Music, and the Rochester Institute of Technology are all in Rochester, a short distance from the inn.

 Shopping opportunities may be found in area antique and craft stores and in the large and extensive Market Place Mall.

 From May through October, the Genesee Country Village sponsors the Highland Gathering, a horse competition, Old Time Fiddler's Fair, and the Antique Fire Apparatus Muster.

 LeRoy airport, five miles from the inn, offers aircraft fuel and service.

How to get there: From Interstate 90, the New York State Thruway, take Exit 47 and North Road to State Route 36. Continue into Mumford. Turn right at the first traffic light onto George Street. The sixth building on the right is the inn.

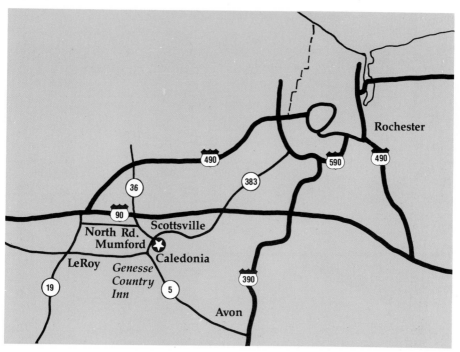

Genessee Country Inn ⬍

The Point ▲   ▼ **Beekman Arms**

BEEKMAN ARMS

Built in 1766 on part of the land granted to Henry Beekman by Queen Ann in 1709, Beekman Arms lays claim to being the oldest inn in America. At the beginning of the Revolution the local militia drilled on the grounds under the direction of Richard Montgomery, a former British army officer. Shortly after the Continental Congress made him a brigadier general, he marched the milita off to invade Canada.

Montgomery was the first of many American heroes, generals, presidents, and other famous people to enjoy the hospitality of the Beekman Arms. Situated in the mid-Hudson Valley where the Sepasco trail met the Kings Highway, the little stone building was for a long time the natural stopover for travelers between New York City and Albany.

Now with thirty rooms, the inn continues to welcome travelers to its authentic atmosphere and memorable dining. The latest acquisition is the Delamater House, designed by the noted architect Alexander Jackson Davis. Just down the street from the inn, it has modern bedroom suites and houses the Delamater Conference Center, a complete facility for business meetings.

Listed on the National Register of Historic Places, and equally convenient for history or scenery, antiques or architecture, the Beekman Arms is at the center of a National Historic District, and in the heart of New York State's first Historic Shorelands area.

Beekman Arms
US Route 9
Rhinebeck, NY 12572

800-553-INNS
In Maryland 800-247-INNS

 Breakfast, lunch, and dinner are served every day. Brunch is served on Sunday.

 Conference groups of up to twenty-five are accommodated in the renovated 1835 Germond House or the Delamater House, both fully equipped with audiovisual aids.

 Public tennis courts are three blocks from the inn.

 Cross-country skiing is available at Dinsmore Golf Course and at Mills Mansion.

 Scenic jogging roads abound, and jogging maps are provided in the guest rooms.

Rhinebeck, New York

 Historic sites nearby are Hyde Park, home of President Franklin D. Roosevelt, and the Vanderbilt mansion.

 Vassar College, Bard College, Marist College, and the Culinary Institute are all nearby.

 A craft fair in June, the Dutchess County Fair in August, and an antique auto show in October are all held at the Dutchess County Fairgrounds one mile from the inn.

 Sky Park Airport, in Red Hook eight miles north of the inn, offers aviation fuel and taxi service.

How to get there: From Interstate 87, the New York State Thruway, cross the Hudson at Poughkeepsie or Kingston, and take US 9 to Rhinebeck. The inn is on US 9 in the center of town.

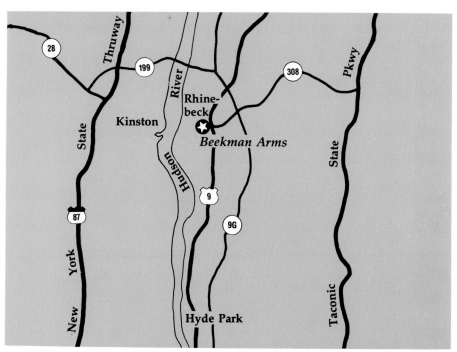

THE POINT

The Point, a private and secluded estate on the shore of Upper Saranac Lake, was built fifty years ago by William Avery Rockefeller as a grand lodge to entertain high society and visiting royalty. Today The Point pampers its paying guests in the old European manner. A stay at The Point is a houseparty in the Adirondacks, or just quiet relaxation.

Huge spruce beams span the large, airy great hall, where giant walk-in fireplaces provide welcome warmth in cool weather. The paneled walls, hung with hunting trophies, have large latticed windows which open to a terrace overlooking the lake through pine and birch trees.

The nine bedrooms, all with custom-made beds, feather comforters, and fireplaces, are located in the main lodge and in other lodges in the compound. Guests share in the fun of staying at one of the last great Adirondack private camps.

The Point   800-553-INNS
Saranac Lake, NY 12983   In Maryland 800-247-INNS

 All meals are complimentary. Continental-style breakfast is delivered to the room. Lunches are picnic style. Formal dinners are celebrated in the great hall.

 All beverages are complimentary. Self-serve bars are open twenty-four hours a day.

 Sailing, windsurfing, power boating, canoeing, and waterskiing are all offered from the inn boathouse on the lake. The inn fleet includes several restored prewar ChrisCrafts.

 Cross-country skiing and ice skating are available at the camp. Winter Olympic facilities at Lake Placid are a short drive from the inn. Big Tupper ski area is twenty-five minutes away.

 Nearby stables offer horseback riding lessons as well as ring and trail riding.

 Adirondack Museum is a short drive from the inn.

Saranac Lake, New York

 Shops in nearby Lake Placid specialize in rustic antiques.

 Lake Placid offers a full schedule of concerts and summer stock theatre productions.

 The oldest winter carnival in the nation is held annually at Lake Placid.

 Adirondack airport, with aviation fuel and rental cars, is twenty minutes from the inn.

How to get there: From Interstate 87, take State Routes 9N and 87 to the town of Saranac Lake. Follow State Route 3 west fifteen miles to the intersection with State Route 30. Go north on State Route 30 six miles to the inn entrance, on the right.

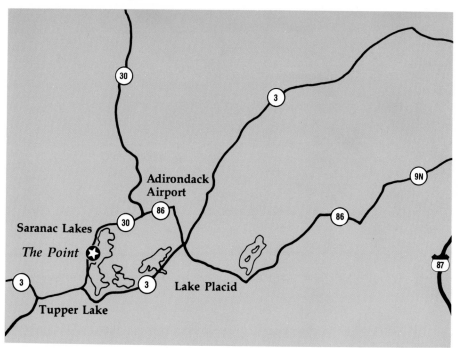

GREEN PARK INN

Situated 4,300 feet above sea level in the Blue Ridge mountains, the Green Park Inn is located in the village of Blowing Rock, which derives its name from an unusual rock formation where air currents from Johns River gorge blow light objects away. The famous Blue Ridge Parkway crosses the nearby mountain crest between Virginia and North Carolina.

The eighty-five-room inn, built in 1885, is one of the South's oldest luxury resorts. The green and white clapboard exterior of the stately Victorian manor house is an intricate latticework, with majestic pinnacles and hand-crafted wooden shutters. The house is accented by a sprawling but graceful open-air porch, featuring rows of carefully crafted columns and the inn's own renowned white wicker furniture.

Ceiling fans and chandeliers grace the lobby, and a multilevel dining room dominates the main floor. The Divide Lounge is named for its precise location astride the Eastern Continental Divide.

Green Park Inn   800-553-INNS
P.O. Box 7   In Maryland 800-247-INNS
Blowing Rock, NC 28605

 Breakfast, lunch, and dinner are served in the main dining room and in the Garden Room.

 The lounge offers beer and wine, and wide-screen television.

 Conference groups of up to 250 can be accommodated.

 Guests may play golf on the course at Blowing Rock Country Club, next to the inn and open May to October.

 Tennis is available at the Blowing Rock Country Club, next to the inn.

 Whitewater rafting and canoeing may be enjoyed on any of the many rivers nearby.

Blowing Rock, North Carolina

 Downhill and cross-country skiing areas are a few minutes from the inn.

 For swimming, the inn has its own pool.

 Tours may be arranged of the high country region, including Grandfather Mountain, Tweetsie Railroad, the Glendale Springs frescoes, and more.

 The shops of Blowing Rock's Main Street offer mountain crafts, antiques, and gifts.

 The inn hosts a dinner theatre each season, and the main dining room offers dining and dancing each Saturday evening.

How to get there: From Interstate 40 at Hickory, follow US 321 north. The inn is on US 321 just outside the town of Blowing Rock.

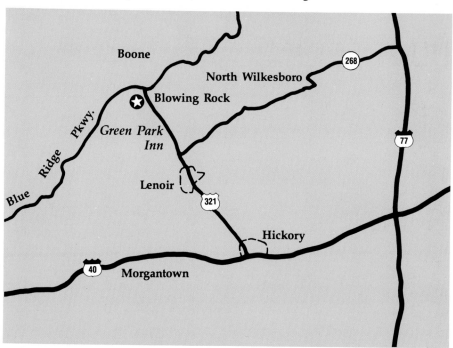

THE LORDS PROPRIETORS' INN

The Lords Proprietors' Inn is comprised of three adjacent restored homes in the Historic District of Edenton, the colonial capital of North Carolina during the first half of the 18th century. Called the South's prettiest town, Edenton has waterfront parks along Albemarle Sound, tree-lined streets flanked by fine 18th century and 19th century homes, and a splendid 1767 courthouse with a green lawn to the water.

The inn's three homes, a part of Edenton's charm, are the White-Bond House, built in 1901 by a prosperous farmer and featuring an elegant entrance hall, the historic Satterfield House, constructed in 1783 and remodeled in 1906, and the South White House, a Queen Ann cottage with peaked roof, named for Mrs. South Carolina White, who owned it early in the century.

The inn has seventeen guest rooms, including two suites, and parlors and dining rooms. All are furnished with antiques and the fine work of local cabinet makers.

The Lords Proprietors' Inn
300 North Broad Street
Edenton, NC 27932

800-553-INNS
In Maryland 800-247-INNS

 A complimentary breakfast of fresh fruit, homemade breads, muffins, and preserves is served each day. Dinner is served to Winter Weekend guests, and complete dining service is provided for conference groups. Several fine restaurants are in and near Edenton.

 Conferences of up to forty auditorium style and twenty around a conference table can be accommodated in Whedbee House.

 Golf may be played at the Chowan Country Club.

 Tennis may be played at lighted town courts three blocks from the inn.

 Fishing is available on Albemarle Sound, in the rivers around Edenton, and on a private lake at Mount Auburn, the inn owners' home.

Edenton, North Carolina

Guests may swim in the lake or in a large waterside pool at Mount Auburn.

Private tours of four historic homes are offered to Winter Weekend guests. The Edenton Historic Commission conducts daily walking tours of the Historic District.

Edenton municipal airport, four miles southeast of the city, offers aviation fuel and rental cars.

How to get there: From US 17 bypass, north of Edenton, follow Virginia Road until it merges with Broad Street. The inn is on the corner of Broad Street and Albemarle Street.

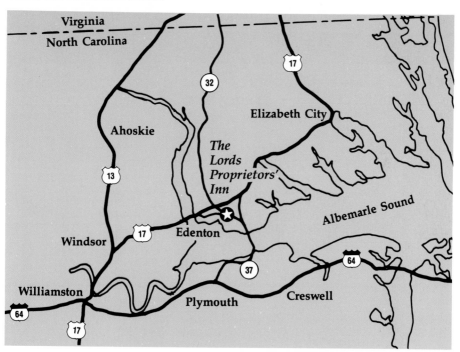

Harmony House Inn **Green Park Inn**

Lords Proprietors' Inn **Sanderling Inn**

SANDERLING INN

Named for a small local waterbird, the Sanderling Inn perches amidst 3,700 acres of natural coastal beauty in the Outer Banks of North Carolina.

Inside, the Grand Gallery and Audubon Room offer the opportunity for relaxed socializing in a setting of porcelains, paintings, antiques, and an extensive library of books and periodicals.

In their suites, guests discover such amenities as imported toiletries, monogrammed bathrobes, fresh fruit, and wine, along with fully equipped kitchens and private porches with breathtaking views.

Next door, guests may dine on regional cuisine made from fresh ingredients served in a restored, former turn-of-the-century life-saving station. The station building, which contains a fine collection of nautical antiques, is on the National Register of Historic Places.

During 1986 and 1987, a summer festival will be held commemorating the 400th anniversary of the discovery of America. Early English colonial and native crafts, food, and entertainment, along with period shops, will be featured.

Sanderling Inn
SR Box 319Y Duck
Kitty Hawk, NC 27949

800-553-INNS
In Maryland 800-247-INNS

 The restaurant is open every day from Memorial Day to Labor Day. Off-season service is limited. Room service is available year round. Catering service is available for groups.

 Wine and beer are served in the restaurant. Liquor set-ups are provided. Full bar service is available by permit for special occasions.

 Conference groups of up to fifty can be accommodated in the inn meeting room.

 Guests may play golf at the Duck Woods Golf Club in Southern Shores, twenty minutes from the inn.

 The inn swimming and racquet club has two enclosed tennis courts. Racquets and balls are available.

 Guests may swim in the ocean or in the club pool across the road from the inn, which includes dressing rooms and a whirlpool bath.

Kitty Hawk, North Carolina

 The inn maintains a fishing pier and boat launching ramp on Currituck Sound. Ocean fishing may be done from the beach in front of the inn. Charter fishing boats are available in Manteo and Wanchese.

 The Wright Brothers Museum is a half hour drive south of the inn. Daily aerial tours may be taken from the historic First Flight Airport.

 Fishing and waterfowl festivals are held throughout the year.

 First Flight Airport offers overnight aircraft parking. Manteo Airport, a hour's drive from the inn, has aviation fuel and rental cars.

How to get there: From Elizabeth City, take US 158 east and south to Kitty Hawk. Turn left at the first traffic light past the Duck Woods Golf Club, and follow the main road north through Duck to the inn.

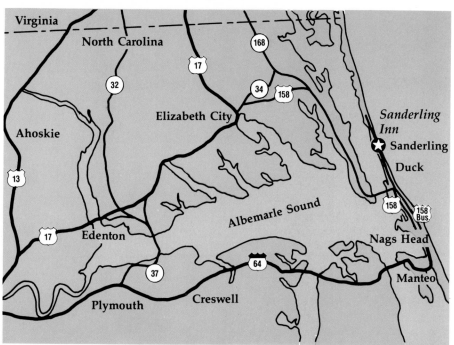

HARMONY HOUSE INN

The locale of New Bern was known by the early Indian inhabitants as Chattawka, or Where The Fish Are Taken Out. The town was founded in 1710 by German Palatines and Swiss colonists who came to America in search of political and religious freedom. The town became the governing center for Royal Governor Tryon and the site of his home, Tryon Palace. Later it become the government center for the state of North Carolina.

Harmony House was originally a two-story four-room Greek Revival house built in 1850 as a home for the family of Benjamin Ellis, a local businessman. As the family grew, so did the house. Rooms were added, porches built and enclosed. Finally, in 1900, the house was sawed in half. The west side was moved nine feet, a new hallway and staircase were built, and four more rooms added.

Today the inn is a Historic Point of Interest, located in the Historic District of New Bern, and within walking distance of many historic sites, including Tryon Palace and Union Point Park.

Harmony House Inn
215 Pollock Street
New Bern, NC 28560

800-553-INNS
In Maryland 800-247-INNS

A full breakfast is served each day buffet style in the dining room. Fine restaurants for lunch and dinner are close by.

For boating, New Bern is located at the confluence of the Trent and Neuse rivers, twenty miles from the intracoastal waterway. Transient boat slips are available in New Bern, and boats may be rented in nearby areas.

Both fresh and salt water fishing are offered in the Trent and Neuse rivers. Lake and stream fishing may be found in the Croatan National Forest. Surf and ocean fishing are within a forty-five minute drive of the inn.

For tours, the Croatan National Forest has lakes, boating, nature trails, and picnic areas.

New Bern, North Carolina

 Walking tours of the Historic District and daily tours of the Tryon Palace government complex are available.

 New Bern hosts an Old Homes Tour and Arts Festival in April, Spring Colonial Living Day in late May, a Labor Day sailing race, Colonial New Bern Days in September, a Chrysanthemum Festival in mid-October, and Tryon Palace Christmas.

 Simmons Nott airport, three miles from the inn, services private airplanes and has rental cars.

How to get there: From US 17 in New Bern, go south on Craven Street one block, then turn left onto Pollock Street. The inn is on the right.

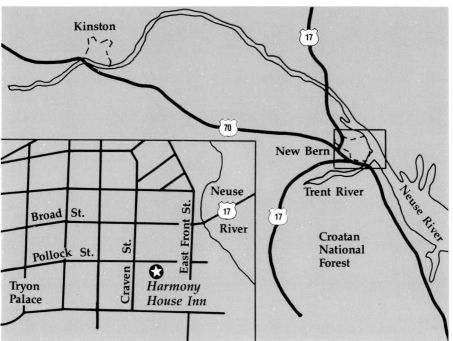

PINE CREST INN

On a wooded knoll just a quarter mile from the heart of the mountain town of Tryon, the Pine Crest Inn is a cluster of nine buildings, a private compound in a secluded and scenic area. The original four buildings were built in 1906 as a sanitarium and converted to an inn in 1918.

Initially a fall/winter/spring resort primarily for devotees of horseback riding, the inn now operates year round. Horseback riding continues to be a major interest bringing travelers to Tryon, along with golf. F. Scott Fitzgerald once occupied a hideaway cottage here.

The inn reflects a variety of styles in its thirty-one rooms. Most have fireplaces, and are located in private cottages, larger cottages with independent accommodations, and in the main inn building. Decor and furnishings range from knotty pine to modern. The dining rooms are done in a rustic mode, with many of the planks in the tables hewn from native polonia trees.

The inn is on the National Register of Historic Places.

Pine Crest Inn   800-553-INNS
P.O. Box 1030   In Maryland 800-247-INNS
Tryon, NC 28782

Three meals are served daily, except during part of January. The cuisine is American-continental.

Beer, wine and cocktails are served every day. The wine list offers an unusually wide selection at reasonable prices.

Conference groups up to twenty may use the inn meeting rooms.

Golf may be played year round at nearby private clubs.

Well-maintained public tennis courts are nearby.

Stables near the inn have horses for both beginners and experienced riders, and offer trail riding, fox hunting, and riding lessons.

Tryon, North Carolina

 The Vanderbilt mansion in Asheville, Biltmore House, is only an hour's drive. The Carl Sandburg home in Flat Rock is a half-hour drive.

 Many shops, galleries, and studios in and near Tryon offer antiques and arts and crafts.

 The Flat Rock Playhouse operates every summer. The Brevard Music Festival, playing most of the summer, is an hour's drive.

How to get there: Leave Interstate 26 at Exit 36, Tryon, and follow State Route 108 west to its merge with US 176 just outside Tryon. Just past the railroad tracks across US 176 in Tryon is the Pine Crest sign.

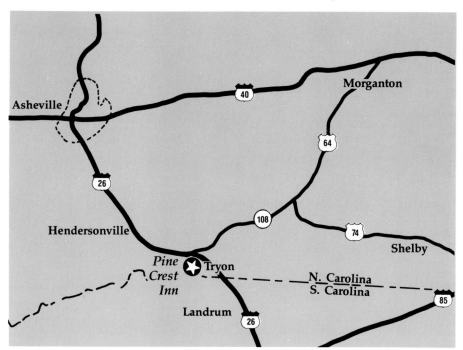

FORSYTH INN

The Forsyth Inn is located in the beautiful Appalachian Mountains of western North Carolina. Built as a two-story private home in the early 1900s, the house was later operated as a lodge for vacationers.

In 1985 the inn was restored, enlarged, and refurbished so that it now reflects the elegance and traditions of finer inns at the turn of the century. The original wood trim, a private elevator, and whirlpool baths in each suite are some of the inn's special features.

The recreational world of the Carolina mountains, with their spectacular scenery, is close at hand. Guests may enjoy these activities, or simply put their feet up on the wrap-around porch rail and enjoy the sunset.

Forsyth Inn
305 Walnut Street
Waynesville, NC 28786

800-553-INNS
In Maryland 800-247-INNS

 Three meals are served daily, and room service is available.

 Full bar service is available.

 For golf, the Springdale Country Club is a half hour drive from the inn.

 Canoeing, kayaking, and white-water rapids are found on the Nantahala river, not far from the inn.

 The Cataloochee ski resort is a twenty-minute drive from the inn.

 Guests may hike along the Appalachian Trail and explore Pisgah National Forest.

Waynesville, North Carolina

 The Cherokee Indian reservation, Biltmore House and gardens, and the Thomas Wolfe house are a short drive from the inn.

 A wide assortment of unusual items is offered by local crafts and antique shops and by the Appalachian Folk Art Center on the Blue Ridge Parkway.

 "Unto These Hills", an outdoor drama about the history of the eastern Cherokee Indians, is performed regularly during the summer.

How to get there: Leave Interstate 40 at Exit 27, the US 19/23 bypass. Go south on US 19/23 bypass ten miles to US 276, the Waynesville/Brevard highway. Go east on US 276 one mile to the inn, on the left.

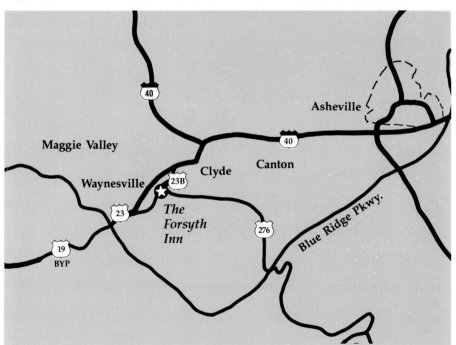

Forsyth Inn ▲   ▼ **Pine Crest Inn**

112

Brookstown Inn

BROOKSTOWN INN

The Brookstown Inn is part of the remarkable transformation of an historic nineteenth century mill into a complex of restaurants, offices, and inn. The Brookstown Mill, as the building housing the inn is known, was built in 1837 as a textile mill for the nearby Moravian town of Salem.

Now listed on the National Register of Historic Places, the mill was the first factory in the South illuminated by electricity.

Many of the original architectural features of the old factory, huge wooden beams and columns, high ceilings, and walls of handmade brick, have been preserved as part of the inn interior.

Each of the forty rooms has handcrafted furnishings accented with fabrics and accessories reminiscent of the period. An additional twelve rooms will be ready by mid-1988.

A short walk from the inn is Old Salem, a nationally acclaimed restoration of the 19th century regional commercial center.

Brookstown Inn   800-553-INNS
200 Brookstown Avenue   In Maryland 800-247-INNS
Winston-Salem, NC 27101

 A complimentary continental-style breakfast featuring Moravian love feast buns, fresh fruit, juices, and coffee is served daily. A full-service restaurant is on the premises, and the Salem Tavern is a half mile away in Old Salem.

 Complimentary wine and cheese are served in the parlor each evening.

 Conference groups up to forty can be accomodated.

 Walking tours of Old Salem are conducted daily, except Christmas and Easter. The Museum of Early Southern Decorative Arts is in Old Salem, and the Southeastern Center for Contemporary Art is open every day.

 Reynolda House, with a gallery of American art, and its formal gardens, splendid year round but exceptional in the spring, are open to the public.

 Winston-Salem is home to Wake Forest University, Salem College and Academy, Winston-Salem State University, and North Carolina School of the Arts. The museum at Wake Forest University features the work of outstanding black artists.

114

Winston-Salem, North Carolina

 Reynolda Village is a notable collection of shops, galleries, and restaurants in a former dairy. Operated by Wake Forest University, it is a fifteen-minute drive from the inn.

 The Stevens Center for the Performing Arts in downtown Winston-Salem is always alive with performing arts presentations by nationally recognized artists as well as by students from the North Carolina School of the Arts.

 Smith-Reynolds airport, three miles from the inn, has full aircraft service and rental cars.

How to get there: Leave Interstate 40 at the Cherry Street exit in downtown Winston-Salem. Go south on Marshall Street, parallel to Cherry. About one half mile, turn left onto Brookstown Avenue. The first building in the mill complex is the inn.

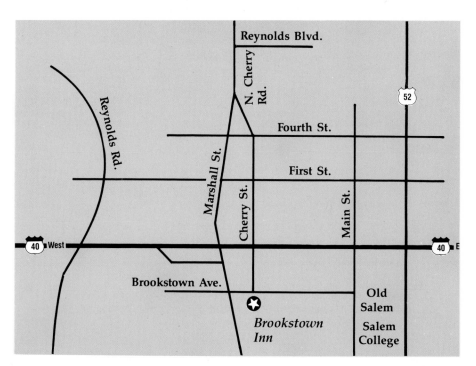

WORTHINGTON INN

The second oldest continuously operating inn in Ohio, the Worthington Inn was built as a stagecoach stop in 1831, and has been in business ever since. The architecture of the inn reflects all its eras, from Federal to Greek Revivial to Victorian.

The inn is furnished with antiques and period pieces spanning the years of the inn's history. The twenty-three guest suites are individually appointed with Sheraton, Hepplewhite, or Victorian pieces. The Presidential suite is especially elegant.

Each of the three restored dining rooms on the main floor feature handcrafted artifacts that complement the styles and periods represented on the menu.

The Grand Ballroom on the upper floor has an opulent cathedral ceiling, a chandelier imported from Czechoslovakia, a glass-enclosed walkway, and a balcony overlooking the village of Worthington.

Worthington Inn   800-533-INNS
649 High Street   In Maryland 800-247-INNS
Worthington, OH 43085

 Continental breakfast with champagne is complimentary. The inn's "white tablecloth" restaurant features Nouvelle Cuisine at lunch and dinner.

 The full-service lounge features vintage wines dispensed from an unusual cruvinet decanter system. The inn wine list has more than eighty international and domestic selections.

 Conference groups up to two hundred can be accommodated in the inn's meeting rooms.

 Golf may be played at Indian Hills Golf Club. The inn is only ten minutes away from Muirfield and Scioto country clubs.

 Sawmill and Westerville athletic clubs, seven minutes away, feature racquetball, tennis, indoor and outdoor swimming pools, weight and exercise rooms, and indoor tracks.

Worthington, Ohio

 The Ohio State University and Otterbein University are ten minutes from the inn. Ohio Wesleyan University is twenty minutes away. All offer an array of cultural and athletic events throughout the year.

 OSU's Don Scott Field is fifteen minutes from the inn, and has aviation fuel and rental cars.

How to get there: From Interstate 71, take Exit 117, State Route 161, west two miles to State Route 23, High Street. The inn is on High Street between 161 and New England Avenue. (From Interstate 270, take Exit 23 southbound on 23.)

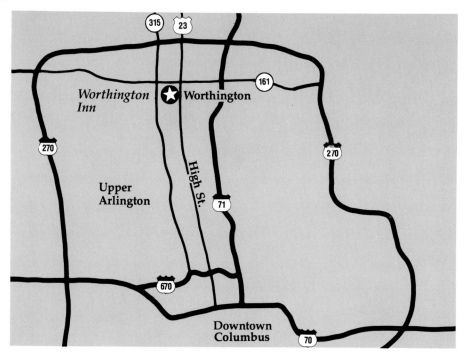

WOOSTER INN

Located half way between Cleveland and Columbus, and just north of the largest Amish settlement in the United States, Wooster is a small, midwestern college town, its atmosphere enhanced by the scenic rolling countryside.

The Wooster Inn was built in 1959 by Robert Wilson and donated to The College of Wooster. Located on the college campus, the inn is a Georgian colonial replica of Wilson's White Plains, New York, summer home, and overlooks the college golf course and the valley where the town is set.

Intended as accommodations for visitors to the town and the college, the inn is a country-style hostelry, combining an early American tradition with modern comforts in its seventeen guest rooms, main dining room, and three small private dining or conference rooms.

Wooster Inn   800-533-INNS
Wayne Avenue and Gasche Street   In Maryland 800-247-INNS
Wooster, OH 44691

 Breakfast, lunch, and dinner are served daily. A complimentary full breakfast is served to overnight guests.

 Wine and beer are served to accompany dinner.

 Conference rooms will accommodate groups up to sixty-four.

 For golfers, the inn overlooks Boles Memorial Golf Course. Also available are double tees, a putting green, a driving range, and clubs for rent. Lessons are given April through November.

 Twelve all-weather tennis courts are within walking distance.

 College health facilities may be used by guests, including a swimming pool, bowling lanes, a weight room, and a running track.

 The inn is on the campus of Wooster College. Evening lectures, musicals, and drama are offered throughout the year.

Wooster, Ohio

Antique, country craft, and furniture shops are abundant in the area, as are factory outlets for Smucker's preserves, Regal cookware, and Wooster paint brushes.

Ohio Light Opera company performs from mid-June to mid-August each summer on the college campus.

Wayne County airport, five miles northeast of Wooster, offers aviation fuel and bus transportation into town.

How to get there: From US 250 bypass, exit at State Route 585 and go south to Wayne Avenue. Turn right and continue around the golf course to the inn.

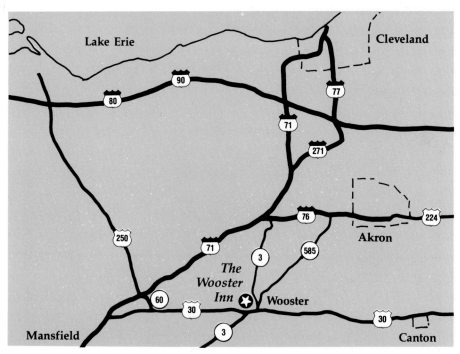

Worthington Inn ▲   ▼ **Wooster Inn**

Inn at Turkey Hill ▲   ▼ **Glasbern**

INN AT TURKEY HILL

The Inn at Turkey Hill is nestled in the rolling hills of central Pennsylvania. It draws its name from the surrounding area, long ago a concentration of turkey farms.

The heart of the inn is the farmhouse, built in 1839. From 1942 until its rebirth as an inn, it was home to the publisher of the Bloomsburg Press-Enterprise newspaper.

The inn houses three dining rooms, each different, the Mural Room, the Stencil Room, and the Greenhouse, which overlooks a landscaped courtyard with a gazebo and a duck pond.

Upstairs in the main house are three guestrooms, each with handpainted linens and window curtains. There are nineteen guestrooms altogether, some with fireplaces and whirlpool baths.   All have handcrafted furnishings, and are decorated in Williamsburg colors.

Inn at Turkey Hill   800-533-INNS
991 Central Road   In Maryland 800-247-INNS
Bloomsburg, PA 17815

 Complimentary continental breakfast is served to guests. Lunch and dinner are served every day. Catering is available for parties, weddings, and other special occasions.

 Full bar service is available.

 Conference groups up to ten can be accommodated in a large suite, and up to thirty-five in a meeting room.

 Golf is available at Mill Race public golf course, twenty minutes from the inn.

 Dogsled races are held in Benton, twenty minutes north, at the end of January.

 Trout fishing is available from Beck's fly fishing school and guide service.

 Bloomsburg University offers a variety of academic and cultural events in session.

Bloomsburg, Pennsylvania

 Bloomsburg Theatre Ensemble offers professional productions year round in the Alvina Krause Theatre.

 Many local fairs are held in spring and summer, culminating the last week of September in the Bloomsburg Fair, the largest in Pennsylvania.

 Bloomsburg municipal airport, a mile south of the inn, has aviation fuel and rental cars.

How to get there: The inn is approximately half way between New York City and the Ohio Border, just south of Interstate 80. Eastbound, take Exit 35, at State Route 487. Westbound, take Exit 35S.

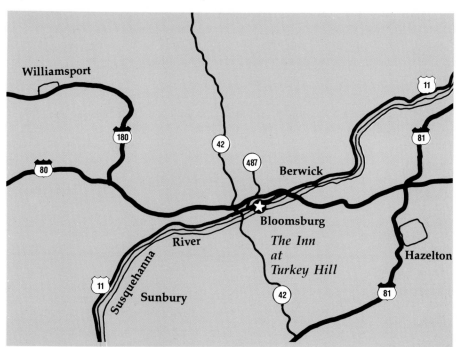

GLASBERN

Glasbern, which means glass barn, is a renovated 19th century farmhouse and bank barn. The original buildings are examples of the enterprise of early German settlers. The barns were called bank barns because earth was banked or mounded on the sides for insulation and protection.

Inside the barn, ponderous hand-hewn beams and stone walls are exposed, and the inn is furnished with period pieces throughout. A sun room off the barn kitchen provides a pastoral view of the miles of rolling hills and orchards surrounding the inn.

In the barn there are twelve guest rooms and in the farmhouse three suites complete with kitchens. Rooms are furnished with king or queen size beds, and some have woodburning stoves.

Glasbern   800-553-INNS
Pack House Road   In Maryland 800-247-INNS
RD 1
Fogelsville, PA 18051

 Complimentary breakfast is served at the inn, and several restaurants for other meals are nearby.

 Conference groups up to ten can be accommodated.

 Cross-country skiing is available near the inn. Downhill ski areas in the Pocono mountains are forty-five minutes away.

 A hot tub and an exercise course are available at the inn.

 Tours are available to the Reading Outlet Center, Strohs Brewery, Hawk Mountain Bird Sanctuary, and other nearby sites.

 Muhlenberg College, Lehigh University, Lafayette College, and Kutztown University offer cultural and sporting events in session.

Fogelsville, Pennsylvania

 Fairs and folk festivals are held throughout the area in summer, including the Musikfest, Kutztown Folk Festival, Allentown Fair, and the Macungie Antique Auto Show.

 Local performers offer community and dinner theatre, concerts, ballet, opera, and chamber music throughout the year.

How to get there: From the northeast extension of the Pennsylvania Turnpike, take Interstate 78/US 22 west to State Route 100 north. Turn left almost immediately onto Main (Tilghman) Street. Then turn right onto North Church Street, and take the right fork onto Pack House Road. The inn is three quarters of a mile after the fork.

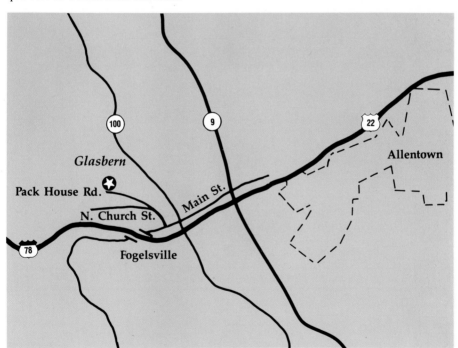

BARLEY SHEAF FARM

Barley Sheaf Farm was once the home of noted playwright George S. Kaufman, and the gathering place for some of the brightest stars of the show world.

Weekend guests included such celebrities as the Marx Brothers, Lillian Hellman, Alexander Woolcott, S. J. Perelman, and Moss Hart.

Built circa 1740 as a fieldstone farmhouse, the building is now a ten-bedroom bed and breakfast inn surrounded by thirty acres of grounds and farmland.

The inn is furnished completely in antiques and period pieces. The random-width floors, Georgian mantlepiece, and recessed window seats further contribute to the early American flavor.

Barley Sheaf Farm   800-553-INNS
P. O. Box 10   In Maryland 800-247-INNS
Holicong, PA 18928

 Guests are served a full farm breakfast. Many excellent restaurants are within a few minutes' drive on both sides of the Delaware river.

 Golf is available at Bucks County Country Club.

 Tennis is available within walking distance.

 The inn's seventy-five-foot junior Olympic pool is open seasonally.

 Horseback riding and lessons are available close by.

 Tours of museums, wineries, and other points of interest are available.

Holicong, Pennsylvania

 Washington's Crossing State Park and Pearl S. Buck's home are nearby.

 Peddlers Village and New Hope both have many antique and country shops.

 Bucks County Playhouse in New Hope is ten minutes away.

 Doylestown airport, six miles southwest, has aviation fuel and rental cars.

How to get there: Barley Sheaf Farm is on U.S. 202 about six miles south of New Hope.

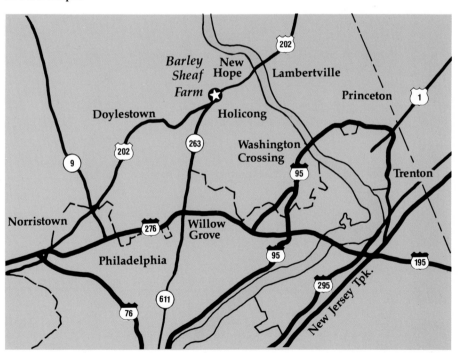

1740 HOUSE

An eighteenth century farmhouse in a quiet woodland setting on the banks of the Delaware River is now the 1740 House.

The inn has twenty-four guest rooms, each with a balcony or terrace overlooking the river and the canal, and appointed with carefully selected early American furnishings.

The dining room also provides views of the river. Privacy and seclusion are a specialty of the inn, although the inn staff is ready to offer suggestions for side trips and excursions.

The inn is located in Bucks County, with its wealth of historic and natural sites to see, including the well-known town of New Hope, seven miles away.

1740 House
River Road
Lumberville, PA 18933

800-553-INNS
In Maryland 800-247-INNS

 A complimentary buffet breakfast is served daily, and dinner by reservation.

 The inn is not licensed to serve liquor, but does provide ice and mixers for guests who bring their own.

 Conference groups up to twenty-two can be accommodated.

 A public golf course is a half hour drive from the inn.

 Private and public tennis courts are a half hour drive from the inn.

 Canoes are available at the inn for exploring the canal when the water level is up.

Lumberville, Pennsylvania

 The inn has a swimming pool overlooking the river.

 Tours of Bucks County by van may be arranged.

 Washington's Crossing historic site is ten miles from the inn.

 The famous Buck's County Playhouse in New Hope is seven miles from the inn.

How to get there: From Interstate 95, take the New Hope/Yardley Exit. Go north on State Route 32. Six and a half miles past the New Hope traffic light is the inn.

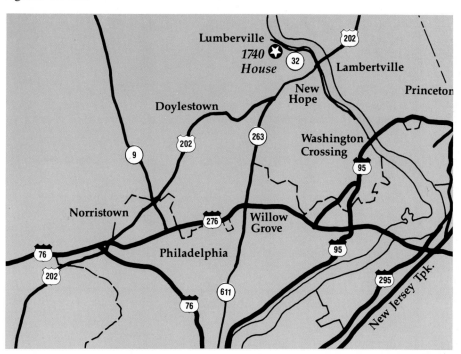

CAMERON ESTATE INN

Situated in the heart of Pennsylvania Dutch country, the Cameron Estate Inn was built in 1805 by John Watson, great grandfather of President McKinley.

The estate, one of the largest on the Susquehanna frontier, later served as the country home of Simon Cameron, Lincoln's first Secretary of War, a four-time Senator, and Ambassador to Russia. The mansion remained in the Cameron family for three generations.

The three-story structure has been carefully restored to bring out its Federal style. It is situated among fifteen wooded and landscaped acres, which include a stocked trout stream flowing beneath an old stone-arch bridge.

Inside, the inn features an elegant parlor and library and an award-winning restaurant offering French and American country cuisine.

The eighteen rooms, individually decorated to take advantage of architectural details, range from baronial suites with working fireplaces and four-poster beds to cozy rooms tucked beneath roof dormers.

The inn is listed on the National Register of Historic Places.

Cameron Estate Inn
Donegal Springs Road
RD 1, P.O. Box 305
Mount Joy, PA 17552

800-553-INNS
In Maryland 800-247-INNS

 Overnight guests are offered a complimentary continental breakfast. The inn dining room, which seats up to seventy-five, serves lunch, dinner, and Sunday brunch.

 Cocktails are served in the enclosed patio adjoining the dining room.

 Conference groups up to sixty can be accommodated in a separate conference building on the grounds.

 A public golf course is a twenty minute drive from the inn.

 Lancaster County offers excellent fresh-water fishing, and guests may fish from the inn's stocked trout stream.

 The innkeeper will arrange guided tours of Lancaster County attractions, and the inn is located near several working vineyards.

 Near the inn are numerous museums, historic buildings, and Hersheypark and Zoo.

Mount Joy, Pennsylvania

 Franklin and Marshall College, Millersville State College, York College, and Harrisburg Area Community College all offer cultural and sports events open to the public.

 Lancaster County has a large concentration of arts and crafts shops, outlet stores, and malls. Also near the inn is Sunday Antiques Capital USA, with 1,500 dealers appearing each Sunday.

 Several large festival events occur throughout the year, including the Pennsylvania Balloon Festival, Bavarian Beer Fest, National Renaissance Fair, many weekend harvest festivals, and the Lebanon Bologna Fest.

 The Marietta/Elizabethtown airport, four miles southwest of the inn, has aviation fuel and taxis.

How to get there: The inn is three miles west of Mount Joy on Donegal Springs Road.

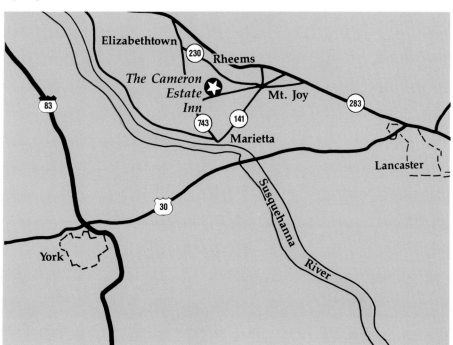

1740 House ▲   ▼ **Meeting Street Inn**

Washington School Inn

MEETING STREET INN

History surrounds you at the Meeting Street Inn, located in Charleston's three-hundred-year-old Historic District. Built in 1871 as a private home, the inn has been many things, even a bicycle shop, before it was rescued and rehabilitated.

Reproduction period furniture and walnut armoires grace the fifty-three rooms. Of special interest are the Lowcountry rice beds. Carvings of rice plants on the beds commemorate the importance of rice plantations to the early Lowcountry economy.

Across the street from the inn is the old City Market, now full of specialty shops, restaurants, and a peddler's market. A special feature of the market is the large selection of straw hats, baskets, trays, and decorations made to order on the spot. The King Street row of antique shops is a block from the inn, and Charleston's historic waterfront is a short stroll.

Meeting Street Inn   800-553-INNS
173 Meeting Street   In Maryland 800-247-INNS
Charlestown, SC 29401

 A complimentary cheesecake breakfast on silver service is offered in guest rooms or in the courtyard. Room service for lunch and dinner is available. Many restaurants are within walking distance.

 Full bar service is available in the lobby, and a complimentary bottle of imported wine is placed in each guest room each day.

 Groups of up to fourteen can be accommodated conference style in the executive meeting suite.

 Golf may be played at Patriots Point golf course, on the waterfront four miles from the inn.

 Horse-drawn carriage tours of the Historic District are available. The Historic Charleston Foundation Tour of homes and gardens is in late March.

 Many historic buildings are within walking distance of the inn, and Fort Sumter, Dock Street Theatre, and many Lowcountry plantations are a short drive away.

Charleston, South Carolina

 Medical University of South Carolina and the historic Citadel, the military college of South Carolina, are in Charleston.

 In addition to the City Market, the inn is surrounded by boutiques, art galleries, and antique shops.

 The Gaillard Auditorium is home to the Charleston Symphony Orchestra and other cultural events.

 The Spoleto Music Festival is an annual event in late May and early June. The Boone Hall Plantation Oyster Festival occurs in mid-January. The Southeastern Wildlife Festival occurs annually in mid-February.

How to get there: From Interstate 26, take the downtown Meeting Street exit. Turn right at the traffic light and go twelve blocks. The inn is on the right.

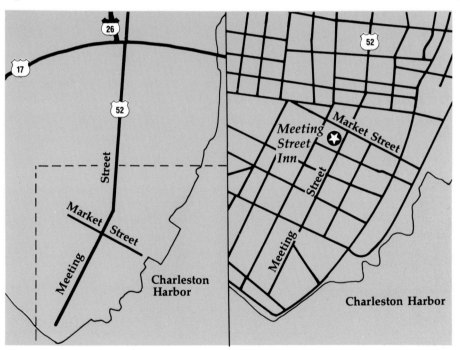

WASHINGTON SCHOOL INN

High in the Wasatch mountains of Utah, Park City was founded as a mining camp and blossomed into a typical western boom town. As the town grew, the need for a schoolhouse led to building the Washington School in 1889. The three-room school served well until the 1930s.

Today, Park City has become an international ski and summer resort, and the schoolhouse an inn. The exterior has been restored, with such distinctive features as a bell tower topped by a flag pole, dormer windows of pediment shape, and large schoolhouse windows.

The inn is an artisan's delight, with hardwoods throughout, hand-etched glass, and many fabrics. Each of the fifteen guest suites is individually appointed.

Now on the Utah Register and the National Register of Historic places, the inn is located in Park City's historic Main Street district, close to restaurants, shops, entertainment, and the ski lifts.

Washington School Inn   800-553-INNS
544 Park Avenue   In Maryland 800-247-INNS
P.O. Box 536
Park City, UT 84060

 In the morning a complimentary full breakfast is served and in the afternoon a high tea or apres ski service is offered. Dining for groups is by arrangement.

 Conference groups up to thirty can be accommodated in the meeting space, which is fully equipped with television monitors, videocassette recorders, and other audiovisual aids.

 Three golf courses are five miles or less from the inn. The Park City course is nestled against the mountains. The Jeremy Ranch Country Club course was designed by Arnold Palmer, and the Park Meadows Country Club course was designed by Jack Nicklaus.

 Indoor and outdoor tennis and racquetball courts are less than a mile away.

 Several reservoirs an hour's drive away offer full water sports, including windsurfing, sailing, and waterskiing.

 Park City is the home of three ski mountains, Park City, Deer Valley, and Park West. Cross-country ski trails and back-country ski bowls are close by. Snowmobiling and ice skating are also available.

Park City, Utah

 A variety of reservoirs and mountain streams for fishing are an hour away. Guides are available.

 An indoor hot tub and sauna are on the inn premises. Full-service health clubs are a mile away.

 Park City hosts a variety of festive events, from World Cup ski races to a Shakespeare festival and an arts festival.

 Heber airport, half an hour's drive south of Park City, has aviation fuel and rental cars available.

How to get there: From Interstate 80, take the Park City exit onto Route 248. Go seven miles to the inn at 544 Park Avenue.

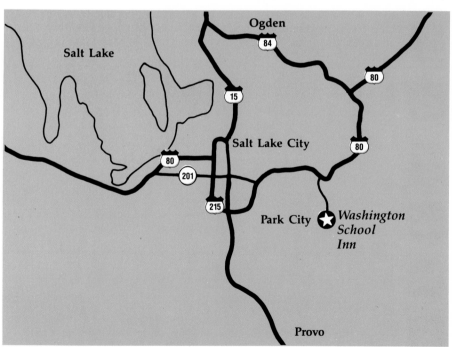

RABBIT HILL INN

Close to the Connecticut River, with glorious views of the White Mountains, Lower Waterford is Vermont's most photographed village, with a picturesque village church, post office, and library.

The Rabbit Hill Inn building now known as the Briar Patch was opened in 1795 as a tavern and general store. The main building was built in 1825 as a home and workshop, and became an inn in 1834 to serve the trade traveling between Portland and Montreal.

At the peak of that trade, one hundred teams a day passed the inn, carrying produce, Fairbanks scales, and maple syrup to the coast, and bringing back spices, molasses, textiles, and general merchandise.

Inside, the inn is a relaxing getaway. Most of the twenty rooms offer moutain views. A comfortable living room and lounge, a book nook, and the dining rooms complete the indoor scene.

Rabbit Hill Inn   800-553-INNS
Lower Waterford, VT 05848   In Maryland 800-247-INNS

 Breakfast and dinner are served every day, featuring homemade breads and desserts freshly baked each day.

 After 5 p.m. cocktails are served in the living room and lounge. The inn's extensive wine list offers more than fifty domestic and imported wines.

 Nearby Moore Lake is ideally suited for sailing or windsurfing, and canoes may be rented from the inn.

 Ice skating and tobogganing are available on the inn premises, and there are cross-country nature trails for skiing and snowshoeing. Rentals and instruction are available.

 River and lake fishing are a short walk from the inn, offering brook trout, large- and small-mouth bass, perch, lake trout, and more.

 Guests may swim in the inn pond or in nearby lakes and streams.

 The inn has nature trails for birdwatchers, photographers, and nature lovers.

Lower Waterford, Vermont

 The inn staff will map out driving tours that include scenic vistas, mountain passes, covered bridges, and ideal picnic spots.

 Historic sites include Saint Johnsbury's Atheneum, Fairbank's Museum and Planetarium, the Maple Museum, and locales in the nearby White Mountain National Forest.

 In the area are many antique stores and shops featuring the work of New England craftsmen.

 Festivals throughout the year include Littleton Summer Street Festival, the Annual Art Show, Moore Lake Trout Tournament, Holiday in the Hills, the Bleeze, and county fairs.

How to get there: From Interstate 93, exit at the junction with State Route 18. Follow that route to Lower Waterford and the inn.

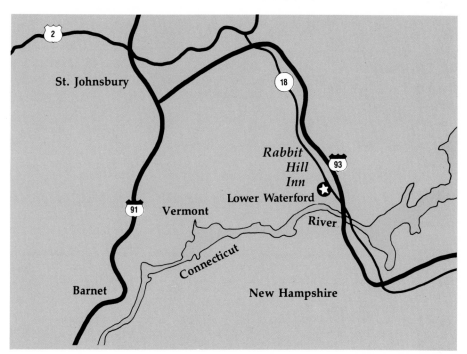

MIDDLEBURY INN

The Middlebury Inn has welcomed wayfarers to Addison County since 1827. Known as the land of milk and honey, this is Robert Frost country, with the Green Mountains rising to the east and the Adirondacks visible to the west. The shire town, Middlebury, is now an attractive college town.

The inn offers fifty-five recently redecorated rooms. Guests may stay in the main inn, in the Porter Mansion, a brick home with a Second Empire mansard roof, a spiral stairway, Palladian window, and imposing porch, or in the attached Hubbard House, serving for a number of years as the Ladies' Library, predecessor to the current public library.

Each building has wide hallways, high ceilings, cozy libraries and sitting areas, and unexpected touches, such as wallpapered sprinkler pipes, hand-cut lampshades, and antique beds.

Guests who wish contemporary accommodations may stay in the Emma Willard House or in the Governor Weeks House.

Dining choices vary with the season. In winter, elegant candlelit buffets are a joy. During warm weather, guests may dine on the wide, sweeping porch and watch the activities on the village green.

MIddlebury Inn   800-553-INNS
P.O. Box 631   In Maryland 800-247-INNS
Middlebury, VT 05753

 Breakfast, lunch, and dinner are served daily in the Founder's Room, Morgan Tavern, or Stewart Library.

 The Morgan Tavern offers full bar service.

 Golf may be played at the Ralph Myhre course on the Middlebury College campus.

 Downhill skiing is available at the Middlebury College Snow Bowl, twelve miles away, or at Blueberry Hill, eighteen miles away. Ice skating is one block from the inn. The inn will organize a maple sugaring hike.

 Open for tour visits are the University of Vermont Morgan horse farm, the Sheldon Museum (Addison County's "attic"), and the Vermont State Craft Center at Frog Hollow.

Middlebury, Vermont

 The inn is located in the historic district, and offers a walking tour book for guests. Architectural styles include Georgian, post-Colonial, Greek Revival, Federal, and Victorian.

 Middlebury College, on the hill overlooking the town, is a small liberal arts college famous for its foreign language programs.

 The Country Peddler, in the inn lobby, offers crafts and antiques. The downtown shopping district has current and antique clothing shops, shops with quilts and leather goods, a country store, and Vermont's most complete bookshop.

 In mid-July, Middlebury hosts the annual Festival on the Green, a week-long program of performing arts.

 Middlebury State Airport is three miles from the inn, and offers aviation fuel and rental cars.

How to get there: From Interstate 87, take Exit 20. Follow State Route 149 to US 4 to State Route 30 north into Middlebury. The inn is located on Court Square on US 7.

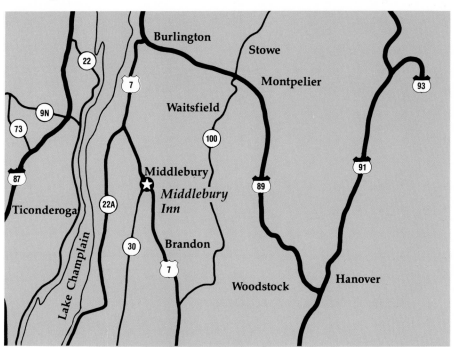

White House of Wilmington ▲   ▼ **Middlebury Inn**

142

White House of Wilmington ▲   ▼ **Waitsfield Inn**

WAITSFIELD INN

The village of Waitsfield, located in Vermont's beautiful Mad River Valley, is surrounded by the spectacular Green Mountains, back-country roads, and winter ski runs and cross-country trails.

The historic Waitsfield Inn was built in 1825, and has been a private home, a meeting house, and a parsonage for the carefully restored first Methodist church next door.

In 1835 a woodshed and a barn were attached. On their lower floors now are the inn's wood-planked fireside lounges, and in their lofts cozy guest rooms.

The inn's sixteen bedrooms are furnished with country antiques, and the beds are covered with handmade comforters. The dining rooms, which are the original five rooms, are small and inviting, where guests often linger after dinner is done.

Waitsfield Inn   800-533-INNS
P.O. Box 969   In Maryland 800-247-INNS
Waitsfield, VT 05673

 The heart of the inn is its restaurant, serving breakfast and dinner. Cuisine is traditional American.

 Full bar service is available in the lounges and dining rooms. Wines from seven countries accompany the dinner menus.

 Conference groups up to forty can be accommodated. Meals and other services for groups are available.

 Six golf courses are within twenty-five miles of the inn. Sugarbush Mountain, five miles away, boasts a course designed by Robert Trent Jones.

 Many tennis courts, indoor and outdoor, private and public, are nearby.

 Very near the inn are Sugarbush and Mad River Glen ski areas. Also nearby are four cross-country ski centers and 100 kilometers of cross-country ski trails.

Waitsfield, Vermont

 Swim in the Mad River, in indoor and outdoor pools on the inn grounds, and in nearby Blueberry Lake.

 Hike the famous Long Trail, which passes five miles from the inn, or several day-hike routes and back country roads nearby.

 Antique stores, boutiques, and specialty shops are within walking distance of the inn.

 A community theatre in Waitsfield, plus visiting companies, stage several productions yearly.

How to get there: Leave Interstate 87, the New York State Thruway, at Exit 23. Follow US 4 east to State Route 100, then go north to Waitsfield. The inn is on 100, just past the intersection with State Route 17.

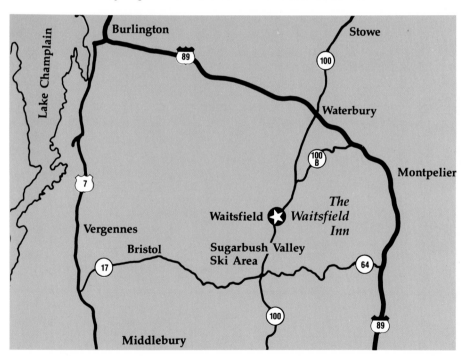

145

WHITE HOUSE OF WILMINGTON

Set on the crest of a high, rolling hill, the White House of Wilmington was built in 1915 by Martin Brown, a New England lumber baron. His guests enjoyed a nine-hole golf course, private bowling alley, and formal gardens.

The twenty-room mansion has many of the original furnishings, including large open fireplace hearths, handcrafted French doors, pillared balconies, hardwood floors, and sweeping staircases, one of which replicates the hidden staircase in Hawthorne's House of Seven Gables.

The inn has three intimate dining rooms, and a four-season patio which overlooks the ski trails and the Mount Snow Valley. The White House Ski Touring Center lies in the heart of a major New England ski area.

The inn's southern Vermont location is ideal for enjoying the many four-season activities there, including historical nature tours and the village of Wilmington with its many attractive shops.

White House of Wilmington   800-553-INNS
State Route 9   In Maryland 800-247-INNS
Wilmington, VT 05363

Breakfast is served daily, as is dinner, for which continental cuisine is served by candlelight and fireside.

Canoeing, sailing, windsurfing, powerboating, and water skiing are available at Lake Whitingham.

The inn touring center has twenty-three kilometres of cross-country trails, and the inn is only fifteen minutes from Mount Snow and Haystack downhill areas.

Swimming may be enjoyed in the inn's sixty-foot outdoor pool, or in Lake Whitingham.

The inn has a health spa with an indoor pool, sauna, whirlpool, steamroom, and tanning bed.

Riding stables, trails, and lessons are one mile away.

Wilmington, Vermont

 The inn is situated on historic Molly Stark Trail, and only thirty minutes from the historic Bennington, Vermont, battlefield and museums.

 Bennington College and Marlboro College, with many year-round cultural events, are thirty minutes away.

 Antiques, Vermont crafts, and maple products all may be found in Wilmington shops.

 The internationally famous Marlboro Music Festival is held during July and August. Many local folk music concerts are held year round.

How to get there: From Interstate 91, take State Route 9 west at Brattleboro. The inn appears on the right, just before the village.

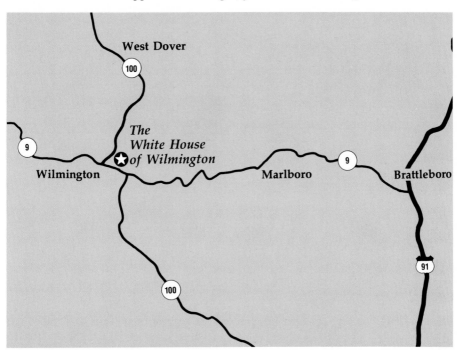

PINK FANCY

St. Croix is a Carribean island twenty-three miles long and six miles wide, and full of contrasts. Arid deserts give way to rolling hills and lush tropical vegetation. Beautiful beaches hug the shore, while ruins of old Danish sugar estates and mills dot the landscape.

Among the old Danish townhouses in the heart of Christiansted stands Pink Fancy, built in 1780 and now listed on the National Register of Historic Places. It became a hotel in 1948, and in the1980s was completely restored and refurbished.

Enhanced by gardens featuring tropical plants and old fountains and walls, the central courtyard features a freshwater pool and the Limetree Bar. Within the walls are secluded garden nooks and airy rooftop areas for sunning or relaxing in the shade of a spreading tree.

The inn offers thirteen rooms in four buildings. Each room is furnished with rattan, West Indian fabrics, and ceiling fans for atmosphere, and air conditioning and kitchenettes for convenience.

Pink Fancy   800-553-INNS
27 Prince Street   In Maryland 800-247-INNS
Christiansted, USVI 00820

Complimentary breakfast is served in the courtyard. Over twenty-five restaurants are a short stroll away, and offer local conch and lobster seafood, as well as French and Danish cuisine.

The Limetree, a self-serve complimentary bar, is in the courtyard.

Fountain Valley, a golf course designed by Robert Trent Jones, is ten miles away.

The Annapolis Sailing School is a block away. Yacht charters and sightseeing trips can be arranged in town.

A freshwater swimming pool is in the courtyard. The sandy beach on the Cay, an island in the middle of Christiansted Harbor, is a three-minute launch ride.

The innkeeper has prepared a booklet suggesting trips around the island, and guided tours by van can be arranged in town. Snorkeling trips to Buck Island leave from the harbor quay.

St. Croix, Virgin Islands

 Christiansted is a National Historic District. Fort Christianvaarn guards the harbor. Whim Greathouse, a restored planter's mansion, is the headquarters of the St. Croix Landmarks Society. The Historic District of Fredricksted is full of Victorian gingerbread houses.

 Duty free shops for goods from all over the world, as well as local arts and crafts shops, are within walking distance of the inn.

 Island Center, five miles away, features local as well as imported music and drama productions.

 Three King's Day Carnival is celebrated on January 6.

How to get there: Take a taxi the first time; the driver will know the way.

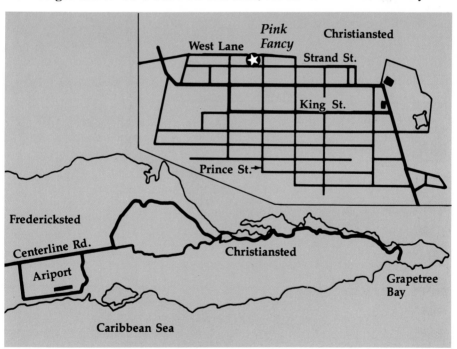

SILVER THATCH INN

LIfe is lively in the central Virginia region of Charlottesville and the hunt country of Albemarle County. It is possible to imagine the spirited discussions when Thomas Jefferson sat down to dinner and a pint with his neighbors James Madison and James Monroe. Jefferson's legacy is still felt in the many local buildings he designed.

The buildings that house the Silver Thatch Inn date to 1780, and Hessian mercenaries quartered there during the Revolution. With later additions made through the years, it served in the early 1800s as a boys' school, and before the Civil War as a tobacco plantation.

In 1984 extensive renovations were done, and public bed and board were offered for the first time. Today, the inn has seven guest suites, with country quilts and American folk art to accent the antique furnishings.

Guests dine in three formal dining rooms amidst colonial decor, with candles, fresh flowers, and music setting the tone.

Silver Thatch Inn   800-553-INNS
3001 Hollymead Road   In Maryland 800-247-INNS
Charlottesville, VA 22901

 Breakfast is served to guests only. Dinner is served to guests and the public on Tuesday through Saturday.

 Full bar service and an award-winning wine list are available in the fireside bar or in the dining room.

 Two nine-hole golf courses are a fifteen-minute drive from the inn.

 The inn has two tennis courts on the grounds.

 Guests may swim in the inn pool.

 Riding for beginners or experts is available at local stables.

Charlottesville, Virginia

 Winery tours are offered by several local vineyards.

 Thomas Jefferson's Monticello, James Monroe's Ashlawn, and many Civil War sites are a thirty-minute drive from the inn.

 The University of Virginia, in the center of Charlottesville, offers many social, cultural, and academic events in session.

 Charlottesville airport, two miles north of the inn, has aviation fuel and rental cars.

How to get there: The inn is on State Route 1520, seven miles north of downtown Charlottesville and one half mile east of US 29.

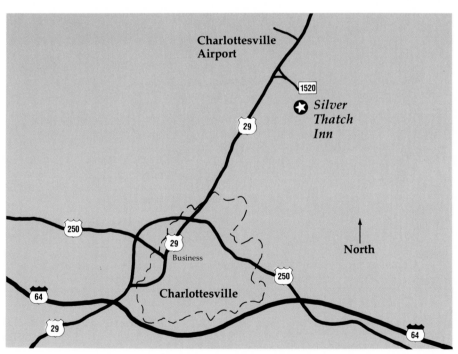

GIBSON HALL INN

Gibson Hall Inn is in the heart of Virginia's hunt country. Built in 1832, the brick mansion was owned by the Gibson family until it was sold and renovated in 1983.

The renovation preserved the historical integrity of the Federal and Greek Revival architecture of the house, yet incorporated modern comforts.

The guest rooms feature twelve-foot-high ceilings, carved woodwork, large windows, and heart-of-pine floors.

The focal point of the inn is the central hall and staircase, with an original oil chandelier evoking memories of an earlier era.

Off the central hall are two parlors and a dining room, each decorated with period furnishings and oriental carpets. All three rooms have working fireplaces.

The garden room offers a quiet retreat and view of the nearby Blue Ridge foothills.

Gibson Hall Inn
P.O. Box 225
Upperville, VA 22176

800-553-INNS
In Maryland 800-247-INNS

 Weekdays, a complimentary continental breakfast is served, and on weekends a hearty country breakfast. Restaurants for other meals may be found in nearby Middleburg.

 Complimentary wine and cheese are served each evening. Several pleasant pubs are in nearby villages.

 Each spring's many horse farm and stable activities include the Upperville Colt and Horse Show, fox hunts, and point-to-point races.

 Local vineyard tours and tastings of Virginia wines are pleasant diversions, as are tours of the local stables.

Upperville, Virginia

 Civil War sites abound in the surrounding counties. Oatlands, a National Trust for Historic Preservation estate, is a short drive. North is Goose Creek Historic and Cultural Conservation District, 10,000 acres, the first large rural historic district.

 Middleburg offers a variety of shops.

 Wine, strawberries, apples, music, and hot-air balloons are the focus of many local fairs and festivals.

How to get there: From Interstate 495, the Washington Beltway, take Interstate 66 west about nine miles to US 50. Continue west on US 50 thirty-two miles to Upperville. The inn is on the right.

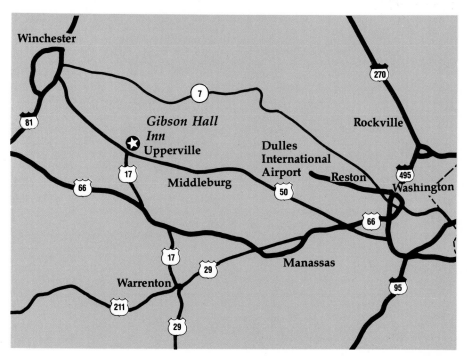

INN AT GRISTMILL SQUARE

The Inn at Gristmill Square is a complex of turn-of-the-century buildings, nestled in a valley of the Allegheny Mountains, that were once a gristmill, hardware store, blacksmith shop, and two private homes.

The five restored buildings now house a country store, the Waterwheel restaurant, and the inn's fourteen guest suites and rooms.

Each room is individually decorated, many with antiques and old prints. Seven have fireplaces, and most have views of the Victorian town of Warm Springs and the nearby mountains.

The 1771 mill grinding wheel, most of the original flooring, and the grain chutes are still in the dining room. Ladderback chairs with rush seats blend into the decor, and table centerpieces are made of local herbs and wildflowers in season. Locally raised trout and a variety of homemade soups are features of the menu.

Inn at Gristmill Square	800-553-INNS
P.O. Box 359	In Maryland 800-247-INNS
Warm Springs, VA 24484	

Complimentary continental breakfast is served to each guest room each morning. The Waterwheel restaurant serves brunch every Sunday, lunch daily from May to November, and dinner every day.

The Simon Kenton Pub, named after a frontier friend of Daniel Boone, serves spirits and beer. A full selection of domestic and imported wines is kept in the old mill cellar.

Conference or banquet groups of up to forty can be accommodated in the Trophy Room.

For golf, the Cascades and Lower Cascades courses are twenty minutes away, and open April through October.

Three tennis courts are on the inn grounds.

The inn has a swimming pool and a sauna.

Fishing is available in stocked streams and with guides.

Warm Springs, Virginia

 Within walking distance of the inn, and open mid-April through October, are the Warm Springs pools with their original 19th-century bathhouses.

 The Country Store and Uptaus Too, an antique shop, are at the inn. Within a five-mile radius are twenty specialty shops.

 From June 30 through September 2, the summer students at Garth Newell Center play chamber music concerts.

How to get there: From Interstate 81 at Staunton take State Route 250 to Route 254 to Buffalo Gap. Go south on Route 42 to Millboro Springs. Then take Route 39 west to Warm Springs. From Interstate 64 at Covington, take US 220 north twenty-five miles to Warm Springs. The inn is on Main Street, one block west of US 220.

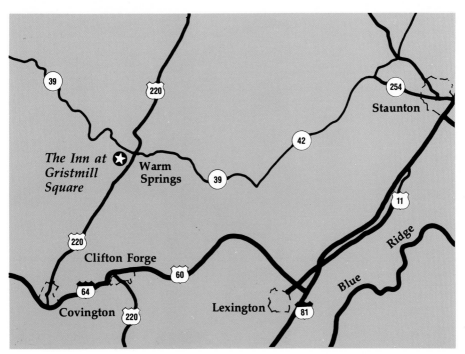

155

Inn at Gristmill Square ◆

156

Silver Thatch Inn

TRILLIUM HOUSE

Trillium House is located in Devil's Knob Village, on the seventeenth fairway of the Wintergreen mountain resort golf course in the majestic Blue Ridge mountains of Virginia.

For a relaxing getaway, the twelve-room inn offers leisurely breakfasts, a large family library, a wood stove, and 10,000 acres of open space.

The inn is close to all the facilities of the recreational resort, and the many year-round activities and facilities of Wintergreen are available to inn guests at standard rates.

The location is ideal for exploring the many historic and natural wonders throughout the Blue Ridge montain area.

Trillium House
P.O. Box 280
Nellysford, VA 22958

800-553-INNS
In Maryland 800-247-INNS

 Complimentary breakfast is served, and evening meals may be arranged. Five restaurants are within the resort.

 Full bar service is available.

 Conference groups up to ten can be accommodated in private rooms.

 Golf may be played on the course that surrounds the inn, and lessons are available.

 Tennis courts and lessons are available.

 Downhill and cross-country skiing are nearby.

 An indoor swimming pool is open year round.

Nellysford, Virginia

 Trails and ring riding are close by, with lessons available.

 Some of Virginia's most historic sites, such as Thomas Jefferson's Monticello, James Monroe's Ashlawn, and Woodrow Wilson's birthplace, are an easy drive.

 The University of Virginia, Sweetbriar College, Mary Baldwin College, Virginia Military Institute, and Washington and Lee College are nearby.

How to get there: Take US 29 and Interstate 64 to Exit 20 at Crozet. Go west on US 250 five miles, then turn left onto State Route 151. Continue on 151 for fourteen miles to State Route 664. Turn right onto 664 and go four and a half miles to the Wintergreen gate. Ask the gate guard for directions to Trillium House.

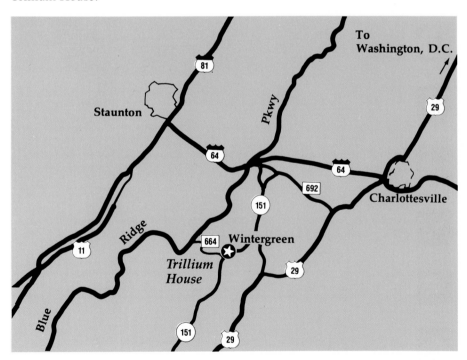

COUNTRY INN

The historic spa of Berkeley Springs, the oldest in the nation, dates from 1748. George Washington built a summer home here to enjoy the curative mineral baths.

In 1932 the Country Inn was built adjacent to the spa to accommodate visitors to the mineral springs and baths. The inn is of brick colonial design, and surrounded by porches and lawns overlooking the village green.

The seventy-two rooms are each decorated differently. There is an art gallery in the lobby, with a collection of framed prints and posters, and an adjoining small country store.

The inn has two dining rooms. The West Virginia Room is a traditional setting, and the Country Garden offers an indoor garden atmosphere.

The fifth finest view in the United States is nearby, a view of Pennsylvania, Maryland, and West Virginia from Prospect Peak.

Country Inn
Berkeley Springs, WV 25411

800-553-INNS
In Maryland 800-247-INNS

 Breakfast, lunch, and dinner are served in both dining rooms. Entertainment is provided on Friday and Saturday evenings.

 A cozy English pub offers full bar service.

 Conference groups up to seventy can be accommodated in the fully equipped meeting rooms, and groups up to ten in the Executive Suite.

 A golf course designed by Robert Trent Jones is at Cacapon State Park, ten miles south of the inn.

 Public tennis courts are three blocks away in the village.

 Boating and fishing may be enjoyed at Cacapon State Park, ten miles south of the inn.

Berkeley Springs, West Virginia

 The English Castle and James Rumsey Museum are near the inn.

 Many antique, craft, and outlet stores are in the village.

 A private airport is six miles north at Hancock, Maryland.

How to get there: Leave Interstate 70 at Route 522 and go south six miles to Berkeley Springs. The inn is in the middle of town.

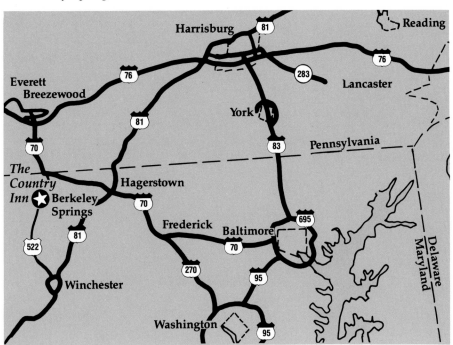

Index